Forty-Five Days to Vung Tau

Bill Mattson

Copyright © 2010 Bill Mattson
All rights reserved.

ISBN: 1449928447
ISBN-13: 9781449928445

For Lenny and Nancy

PREFACE

If you asked ten infantry veterans of the Vietnam War to describe the physical and emotional experience they underwent during their tours, it is almost assured that ten different descriptions would emerge. The following pages constitute this infantry platoon leader's collected thoughts, actions, and emotions, based on six months of service with the First Cavalry Division (Separate) in the Republic of Vietnam, during the period August 14, 1971, to February 3, 1972.

This is an attempt to depict, for those fortunate enough to have remained nonparticipants, the true nature of this war, as seen and experienced by the men on the ground, the grunts.

It should be emphasized that this description is based solely on my experience, in one small region of Vietnam, and essentially at one point in time. So while it presents a true and accurate account to the best of my recollection, it's just one small portion of the whole agonizing picture.

Bill Mattson

ACKNOWLEDGMENTS

I would like to especially thank Lenny Debickero, the younger brother of Dennis, for the time he spent with me and other members of Alpha Company, recounting Dennis's life, and relating how much he looked up to his older brother when they were growing up. It is truly for Lenny and his family that this book was written. They deserve to know what it must have been like for him in Vietnam, how well Dennis served his country, and how he came to give his life in the process.

I would be remiss if I didn't acknowledge the encouragement and helpful comments that my uncle Robert Stansfield provided to me early on in the process of developing this manuscript.

I would also like to thank Richard Beahm for his good memory, helpful comments, and unrelenting pressure to get me to finish the manuscript. Thanks to Chuck Holtz for allowing me to incorporate his poem, "A Soldier's Daydream," in the manuscript, and to Johnny Cook and Jerry Sidio for their helpful comments.

Finally, I would like to thank Jay Miller for the countless hours of graphic design work he spent developing the cover of this book and thanks to Cheri Getchell for her patience, understanding and helpful comments.

1

It was still dark as Bill Mattson walked up a dirt road leading to the supply shack. Alpha Company was out on firebase Charles, preparing to make a combat assault (CA) into War Zone D, an area northeast of Saigon. The second lieutenant was now scheduled to join them.

War Zone D got its name in the 1950s when the French were involved in a similar war. Tacticians drew perpendicular axes through the capital, labeling the quadrants A, B, C, and D. Somehow the labeling survived, even though the French didn't, and now designated the area of operation (AO) of a portion of the First Cavalry Division.

The air was refreshingly cool at this early hour in the morning. The stars overhead were bright, indicating it would be a sunny, hot day, despite the fact that it was still the monsoon season. In the distance, along the green line, mortar rounds could be heard impacting on suspected enemy approaches. Bill was very apprehensive about going to the bush. He dreaded the thought of taking over command of an infantry platoon. Yet that was what he had been trained to do! This apprehension was based, in part, by the fact that Bill was your classic introvert. He was shy to the point of being considered a loner, always lacking confidence when he interacted with others, particularly total strangers. An added dimension for him now, of course, was the very thought of being killed or badly wounded in the prime of his life.

Memories of basic training popped into mind as he walked along the road. He pictured himself and the other trainees, all carrying M-16s, marching to the classes which taught them about VC booby traps and patrolling techniques. He could even hear the cadence caller singing out:

I wanna go to Vietnam
I wanna kill those Charlie Cong

Bent slightly at the waist, unaccustomed to the weight of his rucksack, he softly began to recite the words to yet another song from his training days:

Vietnam, Vietnam, late at night
while you're sleeping, Charlie
Cong comes creepin' around,
Vietnam.

You see the napalm burning, those
it killed and maimed. You pray
that you won't get the same.

You get the warning order, it's
time to make that raid, but then
somebody yells "GRENADE."
Vietnam, Vietnam.

The basic training classes were taught by Vietnam veterans, but it was impossible for the instructors to describe the environment their new recruits would face in just sixteen short weeks. Field problems were made as realistic as possible, but somehow, when a buddy shot you by mistake with his blank-loaded M-16, it was passed over with a joke. There was no way to truly simulate that two-way rifle range called Vietnam.

For Bill, completion of his basic and advanced training meant he had the foundation for continued training in Officer Candidate School. OCS, in six months, was supposed to produce men who could set priorities, think under pressure, and make decisions, whatever the situation. How well these men would perform, though, would not be known until they were placed in the real world. Nothing is as comforting as the four walls of a classroom. True responsibility for men's lives appears as a dim and distant thought. One is always given a second chance to correct mistakes.

Why can't I just spend my tour back here, he thought. Gazing straight ahead, he could now see a dark outline of the shack. That way I could tell Mom and Dad I was assigned a desk job in Bien Hoa. Maybe I should say that anyway. No, if I'm wounded it would come as more of a shock to them. Just have to write that I'm going to the bush.

The tall, skinny second lieutenant had spent about a week in the battalion rear, located on the outskirts of Bien Hoa. New arrivals, whether officers or enlisted, were given this time to get acclimated to their new environment. While it was beneficial to adapt to the hot, humid weather, it created added apprehension too. One had an opportunity to speak to grunts returning from the bush, to see medevac helicopters bringing in the wounded. All of this served to dispel any hope that one's tour would be free of pain and suffering. For Bill, and two other new lieutenants, a briefing at battalion headquarters by an administrative officer during that week made things even more disconcerting. They were informed of battalion policies regarding treatment of civilians, prisoners of war and general matters related to leading their future platoons. The meeting was held in a small office amid many charts and banners. Bill recalled one chart very well because it gave a daily and cumulative account of battalion casualties. He didn't realize it at the time, but when he was assigned to Alpha Company later that day, he became an official member of one of the finest military units in United States history.

The First Cavalry Division has a long and proud tradition. It was established as a permanent division in 1921. However, it can be traced back to 1855 when the Army made Cavalry an official branch. The various Cavalry Regiments participated in the Civil War, the Indian Wars and the Spanish American War. One of the most memorable battles, of course, was at the Little Big Horn in 1876 when LTC George Custer and his Seventh Cavalry met their fate at the hands of the Sioux Indians. However, the First Cavalry Division went on to fight in WWI, WWII, the Korean War and Vietnam. They are often referred to as the "First Team" because, in many instances, they were the first unit to be sent into battle in those wars.

The phrase Garry Owen is actually the name of the marching song of the Seventh Cavalry. The song originated in Ireland but became a favorite of LTC Custer when some of his Irish born men sang it. It was a natural for the cavalry because the beat went well to the rhythm of galloping horses.

Garry Owen became so synonymous with the Seventh Cavalry it was incorporated into the Regimental crest, along with the raised saber. When a soldier in the unit salutes or greets someone, he will often sound off with "Garry Owen."

The First Cavalry's presence in Bien Hoa was not one of occupying a temporary staging area. Buildings were permanent structures made of metal sheets and heavy timber. The exteriors of the First of the Seventh were painted a bright red to set them apart from other units of the Third Brigade. Sandbags covered the roofs and all exposed areas. Each company in the First of the Seventh, Alpha, Bravo, Charlie, Delta and Echo, had similar layouts. This included an orderly room, supply room, billets, showers, and latrines. Most billets contained spring beds, with the showers and latrines separate but nearby. The orderly room was the business office of the company, although a small mailroom and several sleeping quarters normally occupied some of the space. The supply shack served as the storage room for field equipment and weapons, with sleeping quarters for the clerk and armorer. Besides providing a restful night's sleep, the rear meant hot food and a regular shower, the kind you were used to back in the world. Work was essentially an eight-to-five job, with minimal risk of enemy intervention. For those officers and enlisted men assigned to jobs in the battalion rear, war meant fighting boredom more than Charlie Cong. It didn't seem fair that some men got those assignments outright, without having earned them through service in the bush. But then there were many things about Vietnam that didn't seem fair. It was never intended to be fair.

A bourn surrounded the entire brigade, in essence surrounding the city of Bien Hoa. Bunkers and towers were staffed at night when security was most critical. Called the greenline, it served as the boundary between secure and insecure territory. It was not totally uncommon, however, for sappers to breach the line, laying satchel charges on key installations. Outside the bourn the land remained open for miles, making surveillance a little easier. Tiny hamlets dotted the flat, grassy plateaus, stretching out for as far as the eye could see. Numerous bomb craters, extending a mile or so beyond the greenline, made the land look like a lunar landscape from the air. To the southwest, only a few miles from Bien Hoa, was the city of Long Binh. American military presence was very evident here also. Long Binh was a major processing center for soldiers arriving and departing Vietnam. Another conspicuous sight was the military prison, often called LBJ. Saigon was located about ten miles farther southwest. Together the three cities represented a large metropolitan area, a great responsibility for the First Cavalry Division as defender.

It was dangerous to travel north or east from Bien Hoa because little security was available. The small hamlets and rubber plantations throughout the area were not considered safe. Viet Cong, and elements of North Vietnam's Regular Army, operated from jungle positions nearby. It was the mission of the First of the Seventh Battalion, as well as other units of the Third Brigade, to search out and destroy them. Ground reconnaissance was concentrated in an area about thirty miles northeast of Bien Hoa. It was a battleground like nothing the grunts had ever seen before. For the enemy, however, it was like fighting in their own backyard. Hell, it was their own backyard! Charlie Cong operated in small units, taking full advantage of the jungle's concealment to merely hit and run. This tactic was very effective against the larger, more cumbersome American infantry platoons. The most successful GI units proved to be the Ranger teams. These units patterned themselves after the enemy, setting up ambushes along trails or within established bunker positions. The jungle really dictated this guerilla style of warfare. Its triple canopy was almost beyond description. Tall trees, rising high into the sky, comprised one layer. Smaller trees, but more numerous, comprised the second, while vines, shrubs, thorns, and elephant grass made up the third layer. All of this made visibility from the air and ground essentially impossible.

Bill reached the red supply shack and dropped his ruck near the doorway. He bumped his head on the low, overhanging roof walking inside. The interior was completely dark, but he managed to find the supply clerk's room and knocked on his door.

"Sarge, are you awake?" he asked softly. There was no reply.

"Sarge, are you awake?" he asked again. Inside, the sound of someone snoring seemed to muffle his inquiry. Again he knocked, this time with his full fist.

"Who the hell is it?" the clerk said in a tired but disturbed sounding voice.

"It's the LT. I've come to pick up the rest of my gear. Remember?"

"Oh yeah," the clerk replied.

Back in the world a lieutenant was called just that, but in Vietnam the grunts referred to him as LT (Ell Tee).

In a moment the clerk was standing at the opened door, feeling for the light switch. He had told Bill the night before, while they were going over the LT's equipment list, to return in the morning to pick up anything he still needed for the bush. It seems the clerk's motto was: Put off till tomorrow what you can do today.

"What is it you need, LT?" he asked, seemingly a little more awake, but squinting from a shadeless light hanging from the ceiling.

"Actually, just a new poncho. The one you gave me last night is ripped along one edge. I'll wait outside. I want to recheck my ruck."

"Roger that."

Walking back outside, the LT almost tripped on a dog lying near the doorway. How is it I missed you on the way in? he thought. Sure wish I could just lie around in the rear too. There was no activity in the battalion area at this early hour except for a jeep that came racing down the road. Its headlights illuminated the deserted street and company buildings. The powder-dry dirt on the road was kicked up by the wheels, creating a miniature dust storm, just barely visible now. Bill sat down on the stairway of the supply shack and began to inventory his rucksack.

"Are you assigned to this company?"

Looking up, somewhat surprised, he confronted a young man dressed in Bermuda shorts and boony slippers.

"Bill Mattson," the LT replied, rising and extending his hand.

"I'm Tom, Alpha's XO, Garry Owen". Like lieutenant, executive officer was abbreviated when used in conversation.

"Pleased to meet you, Tom. I've been sleeping down the road. Haven't had the opportunity to meet anybody from Alpha."

"I believe you'll be getting the Third Platoon."

"That's my understanding too. The S-3 briefing last week indicated the platoon has been without an LT for some time now."

"LT Matulich had most of those guys before he got hit. Since the First Platoon took heavy losses in the same contact, it was decided to just combine the two platoons. Sergeant Houston, the E-6, has been running the platoon since it was combined."

"Would you believe Matulich was my TAC officer in OCS?" Bill said with some amazement.

"Is that right."

"Yeah."

"He's a hell of a guy, tremendous platoon leader."

"We thought a great deal of him at Benning too so it doesn't surprise me," Bill replied. The LT, for a brief moment, recalled that day in Matulich's office. He stood before the TAC officer at rigid attention, trying to explain why his padlock, which was supposed to have been locked at all times when he wasn't in his room, was now sitting on the TAC officer's desk. It was an obvious security violation. Apparently Bill's explanation was insufficient, for he was ordered to assume the "green chair" position, and hold it for what seemed like an eternity. With knees bent and arms held out straight, he had to repeat over and over, "I will not commit a security violation ever again."

"Well, I want to wish you the best, Bill," Tom said, extending his hand.

"What's it really like out there, Tom?" Bill asked with a noticeable bit of worry written on his face.

"You'll do OK. Mark my word."

"Thanks. I hope you're right." Bill couldn't help but think the XO was just trying to ease the obvious anxiety with that response.

Tom, with soap in hand and a towel draped over his bare shoulder, began walking toward the shower. The supply clerk appeared at the same time carrying a brand-new poncho.

"Here you go, LT," he said. "This should keep you fairly dry."

"Oh, thanks," Bill replied somewhat absentmindedly.

"Hey, how 'bout taking the mail out with you?" Tom yelled from the front door of the shower.

"Sure, where is it?"

"In the orderly room," Tom replied.

"OK."

It wasn't long before Bill had everything put away. With a last bit of reassurance from the supply clerk, he headed toward the log pad, the landing area used by the logistics helicopters. Rucksack slung over his shoulders, he carried his M-16 in one hand and a red mailbag in the other.

Tom had twenty-five days left on his tour in Vietnam. Most of his eight months in country was spent as an infantry platoon leader. His soft voice, somber attitude, and serious mind described the nature of most of the men, officers and enlisted, who had been exposed to the gruesome reality of Vietnam. The sights and sounds of this war were so ingrained in their conscious and subconscious minds that conversation concerning any other topic was always sought. Their eyes beamed when someone had news from home. But heads hung low in grief and anger when news of the death of a fellow grunt was received. These guys lived, worked, slept, and prayed together, for endless months in the bush. When suddenly one was killed, it seemed a part of everyone died. Tom, like all the other "short timers" in the battalion rear, went to sleep each night counting the days remaining on his tour. But he also dreamed of those moments in the bush when a life-or-death situation was at hand, when it was he alone who had to make the correct decision. These were the situations the classroom couldn't duplicate. The response had to come from within, from an inner strength nurtured by the self-confidence only time and experience could develop. Bill was now following the same footsteps Tom had made eight months earlier. His clean, new uniform, with threads still hanging from the newly sewn-on patches, and polished jungle boots, provided quite a contrast to those of the veteran grunts. His lack of experience and self-confidence would surely be just as noticeable. It was now time for him to listen and observe very carefully. Before he could lead he had to be willing to follow. The successful platoon leader put rank aside and gleaned everything he could from his men. For until the grunts had confidence in their LT, his leadership would be ineffective.

The sun was just rising as Bill reached the log pad. Its bright rays reflected off the metal roof of Headquarters Company across the road. The air was already beginning to warm.

"Good morning, LT."

"Oh, good morning, sir." Bill's eyes caught a glimpse of "railroad bars" on one collar and a cross on the other.

"Are you going out to the firebase?"

"Yes, Chaplain, but only long enough to meet my CO and platoon. I'll be CAing today."

"Sure glad I'm a cook," interjected a soul brother sitting a short distance away. "I go as far as the firebase. Ain't nobody gonna get me into the bush!"

"That's the way it seems to be around here," responded the LT somewhat bitterly. "Some get to stay in the rear. Others get the bush."

"Where are you from back in the world?" the chaplain inquired.

"Connecticut."

Bill leaned his rifle and the mailbag against a chain-link fence that encircled the pad, slipping off his tightly packed ruck at the same time. Where the hell am I gonna put my chow? he pondered momentarily.

"You look like you are new in country, LT."

"Yes sir, a little more than a week."

"Tell me. What's the public's impression of our effort over here now?"

"Well, I think most people believe the GIs are pulling back to defend the major cities. Weekly casualty counts are way down compared to a year or so ago. Troops are already coming home in larger numbers, leaving the South Vietnamese, I guess, to assume more and more of the responsibility."

"Shit," said the cook. "Just wait till ya CA into the bush. You'll wish you were defendin' the major cities."

"Boy. I realize now we're far from just maintaining a defensive posture. Guess a good defense is still a good offense, as they say, huh?"

"I've been out to the bush many times over the past year, LT," said the chaplain. "In fact, I go out several times a week to conduct services. You'll find the men all pull for one another. They'll take care of you too. A person's rank really doesn't mean much when he's new in country."

"The tough thing, sir, is the fact that this war is so political back home. The troops returning aren't heroes. In fact, some of the men have been subjected to jeers and ridicule. We should never have gotten ourselves into this mess."

"Well, the fact is we are here."

"In OCS they taught us to put mission before welfare of the men. But given this situation, Chaplain, I'm not so sure it's the wise thing to do, especially since we'll probably be home for Christmas."

"That's a decision you'll have to make, LT. The lives of the men in your platoon are unquestionably your responsibility. Think through your actions very carefully."

A few more people congregated along the edge of the pad, all presumably going out to the firebase for one reason or another. A dog handler sat down quietly nearby. His dog, however, seemed a little restless.

Is this really true? the LT thought, gazing out over a huge open area behind the small log pad. Am I really here in Vietnam, about to take over a combat unit? What am I going to say? How will I react? Oh, God, please help me.

Smoke from tiny fires far off in the distance seemed to dim the glow of the morning sun as it slowly filled the eastern sky. The distant sound of impacting mortar rounds had finally ceased. Bill continued to talk to the chaplain for a while, hoping it would somehow ease the anxiety within his mind. But the logistics helicopter, called the log bird, came in shortly thereafter, and before long everyone was on board. Firebase Charles was about twenty-five minutes' flying time away.

Sitting next to the door gunner, the LT was afforded a good view of the type of environment he would soon call home. The wind blew very hard against his face. Down below he could see winding streams and rolling hills. The triple canopy jungle seemed endless. Small villages and hamlets popped into view periodically, but for the most part it was just dense jungle. The pilot did a hard bank left at one point during the flight and the LT found himself literally facing straight down to the ground. His hands grasped the seat tightly as he wondered what was keeping him from falling out. There were no seat belts where he was sitting. At times they flew so low the skids just cleared the treetops, making their 80 mph speed seem like 180.

Bill had made a brief visit to the firebase earlier in the week to meet his battalion commander. It gave him the opportunity to see how a firebase was constructed and to observe some of the daily activity. Needless to say, the firebase was not what he expected. He thought it would be a major base camp, not just a clearing in the middle of nowhere. As each day passed, all his wishful thinking was gradually replaced by the stark reality of Vietnam. The heat, remoteness, and downright eeriness were all so very evident.

Charles, named as most all firebases were, for fellow soldiers killed in action, was shaped like a pentagon. A six-foot-high dirt bourn provided the basic design and protection. At each point on the pentagon was built a primary bunker. Timber was used as the main building material, although overhead cover was a combination of steel and sandbags. Side ports afforded good fields of fire to the wood line. Supplementary positions, not quite as well constructed, were located between the primary bunkers. Those were rarely occupied, however. Just outside the bourn were the CA, log and VIP pads.

The CA pad was nothing more than a cleared area, approximately the size of a football field. It could accommodate five helicopters at the same time, and thus served as the area from which assaults were made. The log pad was very easy to recognize. There were always water blivots, riggings, and miscellaneous equipment on it. It was the shipping and receiving section of the firebase.

The VIP pad was the reception area and parking lot for all guests and visitors to the base. It occupied an area just outside the main entrance. The surface of all three pads was hard, packed dirt. Each time an aircraft landed a huge dust storm was created, encompassing the entire base. In the monsoon season the men didn't have to worry about dust. Instead they had to contend with mud, deep enough at times to cover their boots.

Beyond the pads, but completely encircling the base, was triple concertina wire. This circular-shaped roll of wire with barbs attached was psychologically comforting, but enemy sappers were notorious for breaching it. Their small, highly toned bodies would easily slip through.

To minimize the possibility of a breach, light patrols were randomly sent out along the wood line. Mortar fire was occasionally employed also, on a random target basis. In military terms this was called harassing and interdicting fire. The wood line began just a short distance from the wire but remained rather sparse along the outermost edge of the base. Trees were plainly marked by the impact of mortars, machine gun and rifle fire. Inside the perimeter activity never ceased. During the day positions were continually being improved. Everything within the bourn had to be built with a low profile. The grunts provided all the backbreaking construction work from the very beginning. Engineers made measurements and attended to details, but it was always the grunt who shoveled, swung the pick, and strained to position heavy timbers and steel. At night these same men maintained guard, while artillery crews fired defensive targets, called delta tangos. The continual pounding of the 105s and 155s guaranteed sleepless nights, for their fires literally shook the hootches and made one's ears ring.

Hootches on Charles were built to accommodate two men each. They were simply holes dug in the ground about six feet deep and five feet wide. A steel or heavy timber roof was placed over the hole. Sandbags were always placed on top. The purpose was to have sleeping quarters that provided overhead cover from indirect fire. While the bourn provided protection against direct assault and fire, it was the overhead cover that protected the men from Charlie's mortars and rockets. It even provided some protection from the monsoon rains. Inside there was just enough room to place two inflated air mattresses on the ground. But during the rainy season the mattresses would almost float, for the water leaked in to cover the floor. Naturally the hootches could have been improved, even with the limited building materials available. But with so many higher priorities, the comfort of the grunts was all but forgotten.

The tactical operations center (TOC), like the hootches, was built into the ground using heavy timbers. The sandbagged roof was three feet thick. Inside were communication and briefing rooms, as well as sleeping quarters for the battalion commander and his aides. Ammunition storage areas on the firebase were nothing but large holes in the ground. Some had no cover and thus were vulnerable to the indirect fire of Charlie's rockets and mortars. They also presented a hazard to those walking within the firebase at night, for there was little light available to illuminate the walkways. Latrines were little shacks, just like they were back in Bien

Hoa. Empty artillery canisters placed in the bourn at various locations served as urinals. The showers looked like a hangman's platform. Grunts would take a can fitted with a sprinkler at one end, fill it with water, and hang it over their heads. The sprinkler was such that the amount of water draining from the can could be controlled. No one could stay clean for very long, however. During the dry season there was so much dirt blown around by the Chinooks and slicks (Huey helicopters), the men had to resign themselves to having dirt on their faces and in their hair and food. At Charles the dirt had a reddish hue, which made the men look like Indians. In the monsoon season walking around became a real challenge. Aside from the slipping and sliding, jungle boots seemed to weigh a ton from the clinging mud. Since hootches leaked and work outside continued despite the rain, a dry set of fatigues was a rarity.

Despite all the drawbacks, the firebase was truly home away from home for the grunts. Most saw nothing but the bush and firebase for their entire tour. During the short stays on the firebase between missions they could play cards, shoot baskets on a makeshift court, and eat three hot meals a day. The food was usually just as good as that in Bien Hoa, certainly better than the C-rations and LRRPs (long-range reconnaissance patrol) rations carried on combat missions. Another benefit of life on the firebase was the privilege of drinking beer and soda. Movies were even shown on occasion. But drinks were often warm because of shortages of ice, and the electrical load on the overburdened generators sometimes made the simple showing of a movie impossible.

The log bird reached Charles about eight-thirty. It circled high above the firebase for a few minutes before landing on the log pad. The LT jumped out and began walking toward the hootches built for the line company. The time had now come to meet his commanding officer and platoon.

Captain Silver, a West Point graduate, was standing on a small mound of dirt within the hootch area. The men of Alpha Company were moving all about him, preparing for the CA.

"You must be my new LT," the CO said, his eyes surveying Bill from head to toe as the LT approached. "Garry Owen."

"Garry Owen, sir. Yes, I just arrived on the log bird," the LT replied somewhat nervously.

"Sorry I didn't get back to the rear to welcome you. We've been on this mud hole for almost five days now. How are things in Bien Hoa?"

"Fine, sir."

"Are you squared away with all your equipment?"

"Yes. I just took LT Barker's entire ruck. All I need now is some chow."

"Good. Oh, here's your platoon sergeant, Sergeant Houston."

"Hello, Sarge," Bill said, extending his hand.

"Hello LT."

There was a moment of silence after which the platoon sergeant glanced at the CO and then motioned for Bill to sit down.

"I'm going to have Sergeant Houston talk to you about the upcoming mission, LT," Silver said.

"Fine. Huh, who do I give this mail bag to?"

"Just give it to one of the men behind you," Houston replied.

"Well, I'll get back to you in a little while, LT," the CO said, turning in the direction of the TOC.

"OK, sir."

They sat down on the top of a nearby hootch. Sergeant Houston began by describing a little bit about himself and the platoon. The Sarge was in his late twenties and physically very strong. His voice, however, was soft and steady as he described his current and two previous tours in Vietnam. There was no doubt in Bill's mind, listening to him outline some of his experiences, that he would be the LT's right arm for quite some time. In OCS, candidates were told that if they were lucky enough to get an experienced platoon sergeant, they would really have it made. Well, Bill certainly didn't feel he would have it made here, but the adjustment was definitely going to be easier with Sergeant Houston around.

"Hey, how 'bout meetin' some of the men?"

"Sure. I'd like to."

While in Bien Hoa, Bill took the opportunity to write the names of the members of the Third Platoon in his notebook. The names sounded familiar as the sarge introduced each man. However, it was going to take the LT some time to associate fourteen faces and names. Some of the men were cleaning their weapons. Others were packing rucksacks. A few were just sitting around talking with one another. Moving from one to another, Bill could feel the penetration of their eyes. He could guess what they were thinking too. Another new LT. Probably going to be a lifer dud.

An enlisted man usually had a twelve-month tour in the bush. An officer, on the other hand, was normally rotated to the rear after six months. As a result, the grunts had to "break in" at least two LTs during a one-year tour. It was more than two, though, when you consider the LTs who were wounded or, in some cases, relieved of command.

The introductions were cut short when the CO returned from the TOC.

"Meet me in my hootch, LT. I'm going to give you and Simmons an operations order."

"Yes, sir," he crisply replied.

Nodding his thanks to Sergeant Houston, he headed over to the CO's hootch. The whole firebase seemed extremely active now. Bill gazed from one bunker to another. He felt safe within the perimeter, but his stomach turned when he realized in several short hours he'd be in the jungle. The howitzer crews were busy preparing to fire the prep. Chinooks from Sandy Pad back in Bien Hoa were beginning to arrive now too, carrying the daily ration of hot chow and assorted pieces of equipment. Their dual rotor blades created what seemed like gale-force winds across the base. Talk among the grunts was of the upcoming mission. A single bright spot was the fact that Vung Tau was awaiting them on their return. The small city southeast of Saigon on the South China Sea is where one of the Army's R&R centers is located. If the men were afraid, it was difficult to read it on their dirty faces.

The LT felt extremely self-conscious walking across the firebase. He reached the CO's hootch pondering his lack of experience, his total lack of confidence. Stepping down into the small, stuffy hole, he squeezed by a cot above which swung a dimly lit lantern.

"Hello. You must be LT Simmons."

"Yes, that's right," Simmons replied without looking up.

"Bill Mattson. The CO told me to come down here for an operations order."

"Uh huh."

Simmons was intently studying his map so Bill just sat down on an ammo box and pulled out his own map. A moment later the CO came in with several more maps. Together they huddled around one of the AO. Light from the flickering lantern created slow, moving shadows over the shiny acetate paper.

"OK. I'm going to give you guys a five-paragraph operations order. Then I want you to take a look at this intel map."

With his pen and notebook in hand, Bill began copying everything the CO said. He was taught to write operations orders in a five-paragraph format. This included a statement of the mission, the concept of the operation, the support available, the enemy situation, and finally the command and signal arrangements, with the administrative and logistics elements appropriate to the overall mission. Bill didn't know whether the CO always briefed his LTs in this way, or was just doing it this time to help him out.

"Our mission is to continue ground reconnaissance. We're still targeted against the Third Battalion, Thirty-third NVA. There's no new intel available at this time, however. The company will CA at fourteen-hundred hours into golf lima four-two-two-eight-seven-four, which is a three-ship LZ. Order is two, CP, three and mortar. The Third Platoon will secure north to four o'clock, the second from four to eight, and I'll cover the remainder. After everyone is on the ground we'll move into the wood line. LT Thorp will CA from the minibase and link with us momentarily before continuing north. The Second Platoon will move north the next morning and link with Thorp. The Third Platoon will remain with the CP, running light patrols. Charlie Company will be operating four klicks to our southwest. Several Ranger teams will be working well to our east. As I said, there's no intel at this time regarding enemy activity. We'll just have to find out for ourselves. Our push will be five-four-five-three after we hit the ground. For the CA we're using Delta's push, two-four-three-seven. Make sure you guys shack any messages sent out over the horn. I don't want any security violations. I'm three-seven, the Second Platoon is two-two, the Third is four-five, the Fourth is five-eight, and the mortar section is eight-seven. We'll carry a three-day log and receive another on the seventeenth. I'll be on the second bird, first lift. Any questions?"

"How long is the mission?" Bill asked.

"It's scheduled for fifteen days. Then we go to Vung Tau."

"Will LT Thorp and I be moving together after the first day?" Simmons inquired.

"Yeah. I want you guys setting up combined patrol bases and NDPs. At least until we are comfortable with the area."

"Will we be moving from our initial perimeter?" Bill inquired.

"Of course, but how far we move will depend on whether we find anything interesting. If we don't, we'll CA somewhere else. Anything more?"

"No, I don't think so," Bill replied. He jotted down that last bit of information and began rereading what he had already written. Somehow he was beginning to feel a little more relaxed.

"Make sure your men have everything needed for the mission. I don't want you to tell me you forgot something once we've hit the ground."

Captain Silver left the LTs and went back to the TOC. Outside, the grunts were just about finished with the preparation. So too were the howitzer crews. The big guns were all trained on the same LZ, ready to lob eight minutes' worth of artillery shells on it. Delta Company was coming out of the bush today. They would take Alpha's positions on Charles. Golf lima four-two-two-eight-seven-four represented the coordinates on the map where Alpha Company would be inserted. It was a small field in the jungle, large enough to land three helicopters. The intelligence maps gave reference to bunker complexes, trails, and enemy movement. Having studied the most recent one to his satisfaction, Bill left the CO's hootch. The sun seemed awfully bright, making him squint as he walked back to his platoon area. It was hot now too. The air was very humid and had a musty smell to it.

"Sergeant Houston!"

"Yeah."

"I've got a list of the equipment each man should be carrying. I want you to personally check that they are."

"Right."

"I'm going to the mess hall."

Houston took the list, nodded, and went back to what he was doing.

Well, this is it, Bill thought, walking toward a canvas tent called the mess hall. I'm now in command of an infantry platoon and about to make my first CA. God, I hope things go OK.

2

By one-thirty most of Alpha Company had left the protective comfort of the bourn and lay dispersed along the CA pad. The men had only to wait for their transportation to arrive. Most lay still, kind of searching their souls, gathering strength and courage. They were putting their lives on the line once again. While the mission was a company effort, and its success hinged upon the coordination and cooperation of everyone involved, the soul searching was personal. It was a way to find a purpose or reason for going out there again. In the back of everyone's mind was one very basic question. Why did America become involved in this war? Doubts were raised too about our military effectiveness. Vietnam had become a political war, directed by politicians, not the military. How could an army wage war with its hands tied? Was it any wonder, after ten years, we were no closer to victory than we were when it all started? Still other questions clearly and succinctly intimated the futility of it all. Do the South Vietnamese really want us here? Would things be any different (worse) for them under a Communist form of government if that were their destiny? Isn't it enough for America to set an example others may choose to follow? Do we also have to be policemen? Of course there were no answers to these questions. All the grunts would receive were operations orders to continue ground reconnaissance.

Platoon radios were set on Delta Company's push. Yellow One, the name and call sign of the lead helicopter in the assault group, would soon be on station requesting mission status. To ensure an orderly departure, everyone was assigned a particular bird and lift. Since each helicopter could carry five men, it would take three lifts to put Alpha in the bush. If everyone followed instructions, and Charlie were not lying in wait, the insertion would present few, if any, problems.

Air mobility was an essential part of each operation involving the First Cavalry Division. Aircraft of different size and design all had a role to play. The Huey, or slick as it was more commonly known, served in many capacities. It carried men into combat, putting them into areas accessible only from the air. It took wounded out, utilizing jungle penetrators and rigid litters. It brought resupplies of food, water and equipment to needed areas. Finally, it served in an observation capacity, tracking enemy movement, adjusting artillery rounds onto a target and aiding in the search and rescue of downed aircraft. What it lacked in size and strength was made up by its versatility. Pilots were highly skilled. Often they had to hover over one spot for long periods of time, particularly during a medevac. Often too, they had to land in tight LZs, where limbs of surrounding trees were just inches from the main rotor blade. Due to the nature of its work requirements, the Huey was extremely vulnerable to enemy fire. A round fired from an AK-47 rifle could easily bring it down. Thousands of helicopters had been lost in this manner, including medevac helicopters. Either Charlie never heard of, or bothered to adhere to, rules of war as addressed in the Geneva conventions.

While the Huey was in existence long before America's involvement in Vietnam, the Cobra gunship was built especially for this war. Quick and effective air support was needed when an infantry unit encountered the enemy. The jungle was too thick for conventional warfare. Encounters put friend and foe just meters apart. To ensure the safety of the friendly unit, support aircraft had to be fast, accurate in their fire, and dependable. The Cobra gunship scored high marks on all counts. Mounted on the thin, sleek birds were rockets, mini-machine guns and grenade launchers. The mini-guns were capable of firing six thousand rounds per minute with extreme accuracy. Using tracer ammunition, they produced an orange hose of fire. Cruising at 120 mph, the gunships were only minutes from any unit on the ground. Their only limitation was the amount of fuel and ordnance they could carry. This never presented problems, though, for when one had to break for fuel or rearmament, another would take its place. They were on call twenty-four hours a day, three hundred sixty-five days a year. The Cobras serving the First Cav used the call sign Blue Max. To the grunts, though, they were just known as Max.

The Huey had a definite role to play in logistical support. But it was the Chinook that bore the burden of supply and equipment transport. These birds, with their dual rotor blades, almost seemed to defy the laws of aerodynamics as they carried tons of supplies to and from the firebases. The shithooks, as the grunts called them, could alternatively carry up to thirty men at a time.

Jet aircraft, stationed at Bien Hoa Air Base, were available too, if and when ground units requested their help. RASH, the name and call sign of the forward air controller (FAC), coordinated fixed wing air support with the ground units. The jets were capable of dropping napalm or fragmentary bombs, the latter of which weighed as much as five hundred pounds each. RASH was most often called upon to destroy bunker complexes. The enemy was normally so well entrenched and fortified in these complexes, it was suicide for a ground unit to attempt an assault.

The sun's heat was beginning to give Bill a headache as he lay stretched out on the ground. Thoughts about his lack of experience no longer occupied him. Abject fear of the jungles of Vietnam, and what was awaiting Alpha's arrival, seemed to now dominate his thoughts.

Sergeant Houston walked over to his platoon leader and knelt down on one knee. His M-16 was tightly locked under his right shoulder.

"We're all set to go, LT. The men have their required equipment and each knows his lift order."

"Roger that."

"Better wear your steel pot, LT. Charlie Oscar gets upset on CAs if he sees someone without the pot on."

"Thanks, Sarge."

Houston stood up and gazed along the CA pad. A few of his soul brothers a short distance away were doing the dap. The rhythmic patty-cake and flying elbows brought a grin to the LT's face. He raised his eyes toward Houston.

"Where the hell did that originate?"

"The dap?"

"Yeah."

"In Nam, but I'm not sure where."

"Sure is something to watch."

"Some of the brothers have gone five minutes at a time. Helps them relax a little. You know, take their mind off the situation."

"Huh."

"Another thing, LT. Better put a magazine in that '16 before we lift off. Never know what may happen even before we reach the LZ."

"Right, Sarge. I'll do that."

Jesus, just what I needed to hear, Bill thought. Let's see, the lift push is two-four-three-seven. We'll secure the LZ north to four o'clock, then move into the wood line. I'm on the third bird, second lift.

The LT got to his feet and made one last trip inside the bourn. Glancing at his watch, he walked over to the Class Six stand and bought a Dr. Pepper. It was one fifty-five now, with no word as yet from Yellow One. Sipping the cold drink, Bill's thoughts drifted back to that day a few weeks ago when he left Bradley Field in Connecticut. His Mom began to cry. He remembered her crying only one other time in all his twenty-six years. His dad simply shook his hand, wishing him well.

Wonder what they're doing right now? he thought. Could they ever truly fathom what I've gotten myself into here?

"Yellow One's inbound!"

The shout brought the LT back to reality and he ran to his ruck. In the distance a low, steady roar of a group of helicopters could be heard. The noise got louder as men began standing up, putting rucksacks on, placing steel pots on their heads. It was a sound they heard many times before. Each time it seemed to bring the same gloom to their face and fear to their eyes. The LT stood by now, about to observe the first leg of a CA.

Yellow One came in low over the trees, descending quickly, one bird behind the other. Door gunners leaned out over their machine guns, checking for clearance. The birds remained on the ground for about one minute and then took off, leaving in the same manner they had arrived. Artillery crews began firing as the first lift headed toward the LZ. The deafening sound of the huge guns made Bill's headache worse.

It wasn't long before the birds returned. The LT was watching for the third, the one that would take him to the bush. They came in just as before, and soon the second lieutenant was high over the jungle. With his legs dangling out the doorless Huey, Bill leaned back on his rucksack and stared at one of the other slicks flying parallel with him. Call signs, security and planned reactions to situations were racing through his mind. Deep inside he was afraid, but he was now thinking about too many things to be conscious of it. Within ten minutes they reached the LZ. The birds again came in low over the trees on their final approach, guiding on the "goofy grape" smoke grenade that marked the landing point. They settled down into elephant grass covering the small clearing. The men quickly jumped out and moved instinctively to the edge of the wood line. Once on the ground, Bill found it extremely difficult to see everyone. Walking was slow and arduous. After what seemed like an hour, but was really only a few minutes, the LT located all his people and ensured they were covering his planned portion of the LZ. The remainder of the Third Platoon, along with the mortar section, were coming in on the last lift.

"LT! Charlie Oscar wants to talk to you."

"Thanks, Don. This is four-five, go ahead," the LT said.

"Three-seven. Everything OK on your side?"

"Roger. No problem."

"Roger. Out."

Don, Bill's radio transmission operator (RTO), knelt down in the high grass, easing the weight of his ruck somewhat. The grass was about three feet high. Visibility over the LZ was fine, but the trees ringing the field were thick. There was no way to tell if Charlie was hiding in ambush. One could only hope the prep scared off any would-be ambush. The pop of another smoke grenade startled the LT, but it merely signaled the approach of the final lift. The helicopters could now be heard but they still weren't visible.

"LT! Charlie Oscar's on the horn again."

Bill took the phone from his RTO, stretching to catch a glimpse of Yellow One.

"Four-five."

"Roger, three-seven. Once the last lift is on the ground we'll move as planned into the woods, setting up a papa bravo on higher ground."

"Roger. I'll inform my pennies."

"Three-seven out."

There was always a chance Charlie was monitoring the radio transmissions so strict radio procedure had to be followed. Names were never given over the radio, nor were size of units and direction of movement. RTOs carried "whiz wheels," coding devices by which they could transmit vital information without divulging it to the enemy. Often, in their conversation on the radio, the grunts used phonetics. Common were pennies for people, Romeo for radio and bravo

Charlie for bunker complex. Everyone in the company had a line number. Lists were carried by the officers and RTOs. If a name had to be transmitted, the line number was coded and transmitted instead. Coding sheets were changed every day. Old ones were destroyed. They were called shack sheets. The process of coding was called shacking. "Shack our loc and send it to the Charlie Oscar" meant code our location and transmit it to the CO.

Bill was very conscious of the weight of his rucksack as the company began moving off the LZ. The straps were digging into his shoulders. RTOs had the worst of it. They carried basically the same equipment everyone else did plus the twenty-five pound radio.

The LT was to remain with the CP (command post) for the entire mission. This way the CO could observe his new platoon leader and help him adjust to the routine of the bush. The CP consisted of the CO, his field first sergeant (often called Top), his RTOs and an artillery observer, called an FO (forward observer). Sometimes engineers were attached, and they too were considered part of the CP.

Within about ten minutes Alpha was situated on a small hill adjacent to the LZ. The CA had gone very well. All seemed quiet throughout the area. The field first sergeant designated platoon sectors of responsibility, making the patrol base circular in shape. It was about twenty-five meters in diameter. The mortar section remained partly on the LZ, affording them maximum use of their tube. Simmons' Second Platoon was connected on one end with the mortar men and on the other with Bill's platoon. The CP was set up right in the middle.

LT Thorp and the Fourth Platoon were inserted south of the LZ. They reached the rest of the company by late afternoon, pausing only long enough to receive updated information about the mission. The CO called Bill down to meet the platoon leader as he passed through.

Thorp was small compared to Simmons and Mattson. He sported a black, bushy mustache under his boony cap. He had arrived in Vietnam in July. After some brief small talk and a few words of advice from Captain Silver, he was off again, heading north on a specific azimuth. He's very much in command of his platoon, Bill observed with some envy.

Thorp disappeared into the thick jungle, with all but his point and slack men behind him. Hoss was scheduled to move north in the morning. Simmons was given that nickname because of his resemblance to the TV character on *Bonanza*. Dark clouds began building up as the officers walked back inside the perimeter. The men had already begun to put up their hootches. Rain seemed imminent, so Bill thought he'd better do likewise before it was too late. Taking very little time, he tied the four corners of his poncho and its center to some flimsy branches in the middle of the perimeter. Sliding his air mattress underneath, he felt he had a good home for the night.

"That's got to be the worst-looking hootch I've ever seen in my life," the CO said. He had come over to check on the LT's progress. Hoss, now joining him, could do nothing but laugh.

"I think it looks pretty good," the LT replied, trying not to lose face in front of his men.

"You sure that's going to keep you dry?" Hoss asked, still laughing.

"Sure."

Rain began falling lightly soon thereafter, and everyone moved toward their hootches and cover. Sergeant Houston, not far from Bill, was swinging in his hammock under a tightly stretched poncho. The LT's eyes glanced back and forth several times, comparing the two hootches. Doubt about the protective ability of his, now, silly looking home became inescapable. It was too late to do anything about it, though, for the rain came down harder as the evening progressed. Soon water began dripping from all sides of the poncho onto his air mattress. Bill had to make a choice. Either let his feet remain unprotected or the top of his head. The poncho was not long enough to cover all six feet, three inches of him, at least not the way he had put it up. Naturally he chose to keep his head under, and tried to sleep to the chill of wet fatigues and the steady sound of pouring rain.

"LT, wake up. It's time for your guard," the platoon sergeant said softly.

Bill rolled over and peered out at two white eyeballs staring him in the face. Somehow he had managed to doze off and sleep a little during the night.

"Wake up, LT."

"I'm awake. I'm awake," he whispered.

He felt around for his weapon and baseball cap. His luminous watch read five o'clock. It was still pitch dark but not raining. Huge drops continued to fall regularly off the trees surrounding the perimeter. Stumbling around his sorry excuse for a hootch, he managed to follow the platoon sergeant to the guard position.

"Thanks. I'm OK now," Bill said softly.

"Wake me up at first light, LT. I'll get the men up."

"Roger that."

Although Charlie rarely hit a GI unit during the night, particularly when it was set up in a perimeter, guard watch had to be maintained just in case. One man from each platoon was awake at any given hour of the night. Each grunt, including the officers, had to pull guard. Length of watch varied, depending on the number of men in the field. On average, though, it lasted about one and one-half hours. The CP maintained radio watch all night using the same kind of shift.

What a miserable night, Bill thought, shivering in the cool morning air. His fatigues were still wet from the soaking rain. He couldn't see a damn thing. Feeling around with his hands, he located the radio, a machine gun and the claymore clackers, all of which were wet and muddy. A claymore clacker was an electrical device, looking very much like a staple gun. When pressed together, making a clacking sound, it generated three volts of electricity. This was enough to set off an electrical blasting cap placed inside the claymore mine. The mine itself was nothing more than explosive material behind seven hundred steel balls, all tightly encased in a hard plastic shell. When detonated, the steel balls flew out at a high speed, fanning out to cover a wide area. It was a very effective weapon to say the least.

Outside the perimeter it seemed a thousand different sounds could be heard. Raindrops falling from the trees created a false sense of movement. The LT could hear what sounded like the rustle of animals. Birds, lizards, and insects seemed to contribute their own sounds, making guard watch an eerie experience.

If Charlie were three feet away, he thought, I wouldn't even know it. Sitting in one position, afraid to move, he hoped for quick daylight. The trees overhead were so thick the sky could not be seen. Bill could only guess that the storm that brought the rain had passed, although there was no guarantee another wouldn't follow. The way his luck was running, anything seemed possible. He found a steel pot on which to sit, and leaned up against a small tree, feeling it bend somewhat from his weight. He had no trouble staying awake, though, for he soon began imagining someone creeping up on the guard position. At five forty-five the faint morning light seemed to turn the odd-shaped trees into Charlie Cong. Tree limbs became arms and leaves deadly weapons.

> Vietnam, Vietnam, late at night
> while you're sleeping, Charlie
> Cong comes creepin' around,
> Vietnam.

Don't move, he thought, don't even move a muscle. The crashing sound of a falling tree a short distance away made him jump. His heart started pounding so loudly he thought the sound of it would give him away. But by seven o'clock enough light was seeping through the dense vegetation to afford easy movement within the perimeter. Sergeant Houston, without any word from the LT, had already gone around and awakened the men. He walked over to the Third Platoon guard position and found his platoon leader still there.

"It's OK now, LT. Everyone's up. You can go back to your hootch and get some breakfast."

"Thanks, Sarge."

Stiff from his uncomfortable seat, the LT rose to his feet and stretched his arms, back, and legs.

"Man, that was some guard watch, Sarge."

"I felt the same way my first time, LT."

"I swear Charlie was out there."

Houston bent down to check the radio and clackers.

"You never know, LT, maybe he was," the Sarge replied, his smile distinctly absent.

The perimeter was quiet but active now. The men were making breakfast, cleaning muddy weapons and tearing down wet hootches. A few of the grunts talked about the "gooks" they had seen on their guard watch. Bill pulled a can of fruit cocktail from his ruck and hastily gulped it down. He still felt cold. Hot chocolate would taste good, he thought, and proceeded to make some. Sergeant Houston was back at his hootch again. He began packing away his hammock, periodically sipping a canteen cup of coffee he had made earlier.

"Bet you got some leech bites, LT," he said, glancing over to Bill.

"Not even. I feel fine," the LT replied. He too began tearing down his crude abode, though the storm had already done most of it for him.

"Better check anyway. They get under your clothes very easily, especially when you don't wear leech straps." Houston was now smiling the same way he did yesterday when he watched Bill put up his hootch.

Taking off his boots a short time later to ring out his wet socks, Bill noticed two large, black snail-like things on his left leg. Slowly pulling them off, his face wrinkled as he felt the jelly-like leeches between his fingers. Blood flowed from the bites but quickly stopped. He immediately began checking all over his body and was astonished to find another along his belt line. This one was very plump. The LT was definitely learning the hard way how miserable life in the bush could actually be, especially when one didn't know what the hell he was doing. Morale among the men was good despite the rain, mosquitoes, and leeches. The sun was even beginning to burn through the cloud cover. It would more than likely be another hot, humid day. Putting away his gear, Bill thought about the previous night. In spite of his misery and fear he had survived. A chill went through him, though, when he thought of how many more nights, like that one, he would experience while in Vietnam.

3

Shortly after breakfast the CO called Bill over to the CP. He wanted to discuss the particulars of a security patrol his LT would lead. The morning air was muggy. A few lingering raindrops still fell off the trees above them. LT Simmons had just moved out. Instead of linking with Thorp, though, the CO decided to send Hoss due north and have the Fourth Platoon patrol more toward the northwest. Thorp had thus far reported no sign of enemy activity.

"I'd like you to verify our location, Bill. It could very well be we're not exactly where we think we are. At the same time, check the area around us for signs of activity. Things you should be looking for are footprints on trails, broken brush, anything indicating someone has been through here. Sergeant Houston has a lot of experience, so you'll learn by just observing his actions. Don't be afraid to ask him questions."

Laying his M-16 down on the ground, Bill pulled out his notebook and map.

"OK. Let's see. We all agreed yesterday we're set up here," the LT said, pointing to a spot on the CO's map and glancing at his own.

"Right, now take your patrol south. But then make a loop so that you basically move completely around the perimeter. Don't go out too far…maybe a couple hundred meters."

"How many men ordinarily go?"

"Let Houston decide this time."

"Right."

"Make sure you have a gun, radio, and smoke, though."

"Roger," Bill replied, writing all of this down.

Each man in the company carried a standard array of equipment. This included his weapon, several bandoliers of ammunition, three or four smoke grenades, one or two claymore mines with trip flares, steel pot, three or more canteens, poncho, air mattress, rations, and rucksack. Miscellaneous items spread among the men in each platoon were radios, hand grenades, entrenching tools, light anti-tank weapons and machetes. With regard to hand-held weapons, Bill's platoon carried eleven M-16s, two M-60 machine guns and two M-79 grenade launchers. Each machine gunner was teamed with an assistant who carried additional ammunition for the gun. The smoke grenades were used when air support was employed in conjunction with ground operations. Smoke came in different colors, but yellow and purple (goofy grape) were generally chosen because they provided the most contrast in the predominantly green jungle. Claymore mines and trip flares were set outside NDPs (night defensive perimeters) or on trails as automatic ambushes. Entrenching tools were used primarily to dig latrines and dispose of trash. Unlike the two world wars and Korea, there was really no need to dig foxholes with the absence of front lines. Charlie had no tanks, but the light anti-tank weapons were still effective in open areas and against bunker complexes, when a direct hit from a safe distance was possible. The point man carried a machete. He sometimes had to hack his way along as the platoon moved heavy from one patrol base to another.

The LT was a little apprehensive about this patrol. It would quickly test his ability to navigate and interpret signs of activity, in essence, put to the test what he had learned in school. He was somewhat relieved, though, by the apparent absence of Charlie in the AO and the fact that Sergeant Houston would be with him should something develop.

"Sergeant Houston!" Bill spotted him near one of the guard positions. "Charlie Oscar wants me to run a patrol around the perimeter."

"OK, LT, I'll get the first squad ready. It's their turn to run a light."

"Roger. I'll be getting my gear ready."

The men carried very little equipment on light patrols. This facilitated speed, ease of movement and, most importantly, a minimum amount of noise. Furthermore, it was less tiring. But the grunts were exposed to more danger on these patrols. Thus an LT had to devise a system whereby all his men contributed equally to this task. Generally a platoon was comprised of two or more squads, each pretty much identical in strength. As long as the squads took turns patrolling, few complaints were heard. LTs normally left it to the platoon sergeant to keep track of whose turn it was.

Due to the heavy vegetation, patrolling was done in single file. A point man walked out in front of everyone else. His job was to spot Charlie before Charlie spotted him and the patrol. It was, by far, the most dangerous single job. Not too far behind the point man walked the slack man. It was his job to cover the point man should a contact occur. Following them was the body of the patrol. Order was normally platoon leader, RTO, machine gun, and the remaining men. If the platoon sergeant went along, he would normally walk in the rear. The last man did not walk backward, but he certainly had to be sure Charlie was not coming up from behind. The job of point man was assumed by the same man on occasion, but more often it was rotated within the squad.

In a short while the LT was ready to go. Bill decided to carry a steel pot, his M-16, two bandoliers of ammo, three smoke grenades, and a canteen of water, which he attached to his pistol belt.

"Aren't the men taking a steel pot and canteen, Sarge?" Bill asked, gazing at the men as they formed a line behind the platoon sergeant.

"No, we'll be back soon. It's not necessary."

The LT did not respond. There were nine men in total going on the patrol.

"Where do you want me to walk?" Sergeant Houston asked.

"Uh, I'd like to have you walk in front with me," Bill replied, wondering at the same time what the men thought. There was no denying his inexperience. But the CO was right. This was the best way for him to learn, the best way to gain confidence.

The sun was fairly high in the sky when they left. The triple canopy provided quite a bit of shade, though, so the heat wasn't unbearable. Walking along the edge of the LZ south, the yellowish elephant grass provided a sharp contrast to the bright green trees and vines that abounded. The sky was a deep blue, with no clouds to be seen.

"Three-seven, three-seven, four-five, commo check, over."

"Four-five, three-seven, I got you lima chuck. How me, over?"

"Got you same, same. Out."

The RTO, walking behind the platoon sergeant and LT, called the CP. He wanted to be sure the radio was working properly before they had gone too far. Part of the new lingo Bill was gradually learning concerned communications. If radio transmissions were clear and understandable, the RTOs responded to a commo check by saying, "I got you lima chuck," meaning I read you loud and clear. If transmission clarity was less than perfect they responded by saying, "I got you two-by," for example, where four-by was considered loud and clear.

Out in front the point man and slack man were moving at a steady pace, skillfully pushing away limbs and vines. Their heads moved left and right, looking for anything that moved or appeared unnatural. Every so often they glanced back toward Sergeant Houston to get a course correction. The LT held his weapon under his left shoulder, carrying his compass in the right hand. It was impossible to walk in a straight line because of the thick undergrowth. Every bush seemed to have a thorn on it, making the trek even more aggravating.

This damn steel pot! Bill cursed to himself, each time a branch or vine caught the top of it, pushing it down over his eyes. Hell, no wonder the guys don't wear them on patrol.

The men walked about five meters apart. But each time the LT got hung up in thorns or vines the platoon sergeant got farther ahead. Bill soon found it difficult to keep up. The rest of the men seemed to have little difficulty with the vegetation and were always waiting behind their LT.

"How far have we gone, Sarge?" he asked, when the patrol had stopped and Bill was able to catch up. The LT was breathing hard. Houston held up a finger to his mouth, motioning Bill to be quiet.

"Point man thought we had movement out to the front," he whispered a moment later.

"How far have we gone?" the LT asked again, softly.

"About one hundred fifty meters."

Bill didn't really have a good idea, but thought it seemed like more than that. His fatigue shirt was almost completely soaked with sweat.

"Call the CP and tell them we're starting our loop around," Sergeant Houston told the RTO after they had traveled another one hundred fifty meters.

Following a short break they started moving again, bending around to their left. Visibility was no more than ten feet. Navigation by terrain features was all but impossible. An accurate pace count and azimuth were the only ways one could maintain a respectable estimate of location.

The ability of a platoon leader to navigate influenced the amount of confidence and respect he received from his men. This, in turn, dictated how effective his unit was. This very thought remained in the back of the LT's mind as they walked along. Back in the world he had heard about all-American firefights, GIs walking into their own automatic ambushes, all sorts of things that were related to location, map reading ability, and common sense. Having finally seen what the jungles of Vietnam were like, he could understand how easy it was to become lost or disoriented. The training

Bill received in land navigation back in Georgia was realistic and helpful. Candidates were taught how to move by utilizing terrain features and a compass. By recognizing certain hilltops, rivers, and valleys, they could relate them to their representations on the map and thus pinpoint their own location. However, use of terrain features required a certain amount of unobstructed visibility. Vietnam, unfortunately, rarely conformed. Another method had to be employed.

Getting from point A to point B meant following a certain direction (or directions) for a certain distance. Direction was maintained by following the arrow of a compass. Distance was measured by counting the number of steps (paces) from the point of departure. This was the only feasible way to move in much of Vietnam. In general it was quite reliable, even though there were things working against the men. One handicap was the fact that they couldn't walk in a straight line. The vegetation was just too thick. Furthermore, a point man always tended to stray one particular way, so the LT, or whoever had the compass up front, had to keep him constantly on course as best he could. Since hills had to be climbed, rivers crossed, and vegetation trampled, pace counts were going to be somewhat unreliable. Outdated maps created another handicap. Locations of rivers didn't coincide with those pictured on the map, while some open areas depicted on the map had become overgrown, thus nonexistent. Many logging roads in the AO presented the same problem. Some were old and overgrown. Others were too new to even appear on the map. To keep error to a minimum, direction was checked often, by several men, each with his own compass. Two or three men maintained a pace count, and an average was usually assumed correct. The LTs, however, were also taught to request help if ever in doubt about their location. There were many ways to become oriented once again, including the use of artillery rounds fired on a certain grid coordinate or a rifle fired from a known location. "Jungle commo" was sometimes used when two or more friendly units were moving close to one another. By banging a steel pot against a tree, one unit could divulge its location to the others, without telling the world. These techniques were widely used in Vietnam.

The RTO again called the CP when the patrol was about fifty meters from the perimeter, ensuring all knew they were coming in. The men filed in the same way they had left. The sun was really beating down by this time. Noticing the battalion commander talking with the CO, Bill decided to wait and report his negative findings after the colonel departed. While on patrol he heard a helicopter land in the vicinity of their perimeter, but didn't know what to make of it. He was unaware that battalion commanders made frequent visits to the bush, sometimes to relate pertinent information, other times just to observe the operation firsthand.

"How are things going?" the colonel asked, recognizing Bill as the LT walked toward his hootch.

"Oh, I've got a lot to learn, sir. But one thing is certain. I'm not acclimated yet." Sweat was pouring down Bill's face and into his eyes.

"You'll get used to it, don't worry."

"I hope so."

The patrol had taken everything out of Bill. He actually felt weak and sick to his stomach. Lying down in the shade, he sipped water from his canteen and reflected on the events of the day. How could the United States ever hope to win the war for the South Vietnamese with these conditions? he thought. What a hell of a place to fight a war!

On the west side of the LZ, about one hundred meters from their perimeter, a large, slow-moving stream wound its way south. In the late afternoon the men took advantage of this and replenished their water supply. Although the stream was clear, the LT made sure they dropped a couple of iodine tablets into each canteen. None of the men cared for the taste of the water once it was purified, so they generally poured Kool-Aid in too. The only trouble was it sweetened the water and made them want to drink even more. Bill had secured both banks of the stream with men from his eight-man water patrol. He didn't think it unreasonable, then, to let some of his men take a bath. Most still had a tinge of red on their skin from Charles. This provided them with a fine opportunity to really wash if off. Darkness set in a short time later and once again they all settled down for another night in the jungles of Vietnam.

4

"LT, a few of the men in the mortar section heard movement north of their position," the CO said. "I want you to take a patrol out and see what you can find."

It was about midmorning of the following day. You're kidding, Bill thought. Walk right out there into something waiting for us?

"Do you understand, LT?" Bill stood there with a puzzled look on his face.

"Uh, yes, sir. I'll check it out right now."

For the first time since the CA, Bill's fear had surfaced and was now clearly written on his face. Is it wise to go out now? he pondered. Shouldn't we just stay down and wait it out? This thought was quickly suppressed, though, and he soon found himself walking third man in a seven-man recon patrol, carefully sweeping an area where the movement was last heard. The patrol searched for thirty minutes without finding any indications that man or animal had been in the vicinity of the LZ.

Three days had passed since the CA. Alpha Company could find no signs of enemy activity in the AO. This was comforting in one sense, but it created problems also. The men were becoming lax to the whole situation. They acted as though the enemy no longer existed by failing to maintain a constant state of alertness while in the perimeter, forgetting about noise discipline, and bitching about everything. It was a very serious problem, one that the LT was made aware of long before coming to Vietnam. The solution called for increased and constant supervision, with motivation not only coming from the platoon leader, but the platoon sergeant and squad leaders as well. Theirs was a difficult job, for as much as they wanted to be one of the guys, they couldn't. They had to accomplish the mission and ensure the safety of their men in the process. Bill countered the apathy by keeping his men busy. He ordered weapons cleaned and re-cleaned. His men cut fields of fire for the machine gun and modified portions of the perimeter to provide better all-around security. Bill personally supervised the medic's weekly distribution of malaria pills. A few of his men had the habit of not taking them, hoping, of course, to come down with the disease. They would gladly trade the periodic attacks of chills and fever for one less month in the bush. The worst part of the mission up to this point for Bill was the misery associated with the monsoon season. Much of the dissatisfaction exhibited by his men actually stemmed from the same thing. It was raining two or three times a day, often through the night. The mosquito and leech problem was exacerbated during this wet weather, almost to the point of being unbearable. Hacking and coughing were common at night. It was impossible to stay completely dry. The grunts slept under mosquito nets but had no protection during guard. It seemed as though the mosquitoes knew this and were just waiting at the guard positions each night. Leeches were continuously picked off ankles and waists, most often after returning from a patrol, and particularly when streams had been crossed along the way. No matter how tightly boots were laced or belts tied, the grunts got bitten.

The streams and rivers encountered on patrol were generally small and fairly easy to ford. Seldom was the depth above the waist. But when it was, another crossing point was sought. Security always presented problems when danger areas such as a river had to be negotiated. A machine gun was brought up and positioned on the near bank, facing the far side. One or two men were sent upstream a short distance, while the same number moved downstream a few meters. The LT then sent his point man across, covering him as best he could. Once the point man reached the other side and quickly checked the area, another man was sent across, and so on, until the entire patrol was across. A river was considered a danger area because it was open, with good fields of fire up and down. If care was not exercised, it was a very good place to get ambushed.

Bill found the heat of the day bothering him less and less, for it was just a matter of adjusting to the climate. The week they gave him in Bien Hoa just wasn't enough. There's a big difference between lying around in the heat and working in it. His water consumption began to decrease too. He had been drinking twice as much as anyone else, characteristic of men new in country. Time was passing very quickly. Log day had arrived. The log bird touched down on the LZ about noon. Along with a resupply of food, which included nine gallons of ice cream, the men got their midmonth pay from the XO. They also had a brief religious service from the same chaplain Bill met on the log pad that first morning. It was a service quite different from any the LT ever had back in the world. Scriptures were read from well-worn, mud-caked books, with M-16s lying just inches away in case the worst should happen at that moment.

With the log came word they would be moving to a new location the next day. The mission remained the same. But battalion was hopeful they would find indications of enemy activity this time. Bill, in truth, did not share this hope. He kept wishing they would never find the enemy.

Our scheduled lift is at zero nine-thirty," the CO said, talking with the LT that night. "We'll be inserted closer to the Second and Fourth platoons. You'll be running light patrols out from the CP just as you have been here. Hoss and Wes will continue working to our north."

"Any intel in the area?"

"No, Bill, nothing whatsoever."

At dawn the men began packing their gear, anxious to leave because it meant a change of scene and routine. Yet they were anxious too about their new home.

"The weather's good, Chuck. I expect Yellow One will be on schedule."

"Forget about the birds being on time, LT. I've been out here for eight months and have never known them to come in when they say they are. We always end up waiting. They never wait on us."

"I'll take your word for it." he replied, smiling.

Bill was sitting with Chuck Holtz, one of his squad leaders, listening for the familiar sound of helicopters. Finally, at eleven-thirty, they arrived. They were only two hours late. The men moved out in a somewhat disorderly manner but hit a green (safe) LZ, much to their comfort.

Moving north into the wood line, they quickly, but methodically, set up their perimeter. Each man was placed in position by his squad leader, until both squads were linked, forming an almost perfect circle. Once given a place on the perimeter, the first thing each man did was run a claymore mine out from his individual position. At the guard positions, which normally covered trails or any likely avenues of approach, at least two, if not more, claymores were set out. This was, of course, in addition to the machine guns, which were always placed there. Meanwhile, inside the perimeter, the RTOs were setting up communications with the Second and Fourth platoons, as well as battalion. Once these things were accomplished, work on improving the individual positions began. This priority of work was done every day so it was something the grunts did automatically.

Bill took a patrol out once the forward operating base, as it was sometimes called, was established. They reconnoitered all around their perimeter, discovering a stream about one hundred eighty-five meters to the east. This was important because it meant they had a readily available supply of water, just as they did at their previous location. It was foolish to waste valuable blade time calling for a resupply when stream water was just as good. When there weren't streams available, though, a resupply had to be called in regularly. Since helicopters couldn't always land and unload, often they just hovered over an area designated by the platoon leader for the "kick out," and dropped the water to the platoon. The water was placed in large rubber bags, called elephant rubbers by the grunts, and these in turn were placed inside empty artillery canisters. The canisters absorbed the shock of the drop and generally left the rubber bags unbroken. The only hazard about the entire operation was the possibility of one of the canisters falling on someone.

The vegetation was just as thick as before, with bamboo trees covering the area as well. The perimeter was constructed within a group of these trees. Old C-ration cans and LRRP bags on the ground indicated other GI units had worked this area before. The grunts were always careless and lazy when it came to the proper disposal of trash. None of the other units in the battalion were any different in this regard, so Bill wasn't about to try to change what seemed like an unwritten policy. From a tactical point of view, however, this was unacceptable behavior. By throwing litter on the ground as they did, Charlie could easily track their movement. He could tell, almost to the man, how many GIs were in the unit and when they had passed through the area. He was also known to be a scavenger, eating what the grunts threw away. By not burying their trash, or taking it with them, the grunts were informing Charlie and feeding him at the same time.

Late in the afternoon a heavy thundershower fell. Bill was able to collect enough water, running off his now more soundly erected poncho, to wash his hair. His hootches were actually looking good these days. More importantly, they were keeping him fairly dry. He still received comments from the CO and his men about the construction work, but he always managed to laugh along with them. The secret, which took him a while to learn, was to make sure, first of all, that the plastic poncho was free of holes. Then it had to be stretched and tied tightly at all four corners to ensure there were no pockets for water to accumulate.

Finally, it had to be tied in the middle to a branch that kept the midpoint above the four corners. In other words, if the end result looked like the roof of a house you were in good shape. While the new ponchos were generally free of leaks, some of the older ones (and many of the men were using older ones) had tiny holes in a number of places. These had to be patched as best as possible. Shoe laces were used to tie the poncho to the branches. But they gradually rotted from all the humidity and wet weather. The grunts really had to improvise. Sleeping on the ground wasn't too bad if you were lucky to have an air mattress free of leaks. The unlucky ones were just lying on a piece of plastic by morning. Some of the men had hammocks. But they had the difficult task, particularly if they weren't in a leadership position, of finding two trees that were the correct size and proper distance apart.

Bill's men bitched and complained the next morning when the LT told them to dig a latrine. Still they didn't hesitate in doing a good job. The CO planned on staying in this location for three or four days. It was important to maintain good field sanitation habits. Bill knew his men believed this also. They just needed something to complain about. The LT was gradually gaining confidence in himself and his ability to handle the routine. The men never stopped complaining, but he felt he was gaining their respect. They always did what he told them to do, no matter how time consuming or laborious the task.

"Would you like to help me fire some DTs tonight, Bill?" the FO asked while Bill was eating his supper.

"I sure would, Butch. I could use the experience." Bill gestured for Butch to join him. The FO was a first lieutenant in the artillery and traveled with Alpha Company on its missions. Although his commander was back at the firebase, Butch reported directly to Captain Silver. He was responsible for all artillery support requested by the company.

"We'll be firing them about eight o'clock," he said, sitting down on Bill's steel pot.

"OK, fine."

"So how do you like the bush?"

"I'm getting used to it," Bill replied, offering him one of the two candy bars he had saved for dessert.

"Oh, thanks...I really hate it out here. Hopefully I can get a job on the firebase soon."

"I know what you mean, Butch." Bill gazed out along the now dark perimeter as the FO got up and headed back to his hootch.

Shortly before eight o'clock they got together again. Butch went over the procedure they would follow.

"They'll be firing a Wilson Pickett round first. What you have to do, Bill, is count the number of seconds between flash and bang. Multiply this by three hundred fifty meters gives you the distance to impact. Wilson Pickett is the phonetic term for white phosphorous. The WP is always fired initially in the event the round is off target and lands on a friendly position. It won't cause the casualties a high explosive round would inflict. Furthermore, the WP round is timed so that it will explode in the air, making it visible to units on the ground. Since light travels faster than sound, the bright flash is seen before one hears the sound of the explosion. It's like judging how far a thunderstorm is from your location, Bill. You merely count the number of seconds between the flash of lightning and the sound of thunder."

"Do you call in HE once you're sure of this distance?"

"Right, and bring it in as close as you want, normally dropping one hundred meters at a time."

It wasn't long before Butch got the go-ahead from battalion and the two LTs called in the fire mission. The rounds initially impacted one thousand meters out, but were brought to within six hundred meters of their position. Any closer and the men would have received shrapnel. Even at six hundred meters, the LTs heard pieces of metal whizzing through the treetops over their heads. Within twenty minutes the mission was complete. The LTs said good night to one another and departed. It was a very dark night. Bill had a little trouble finding his way back to his hootch. Having found it, he removed his boots and crawled under the poncho. He drifted off to sleep reflecting on the events of the day and the mission thus far.

"LT, wake up, it's time for your guard," Don Lloyd said, gently poking the LT. Bill rolled over and looked at his watch. It was eleven-thirty, seemingly only minutes after he had fallen asleep.

"I'm supposed to have last guard," he told his RTO.

"They just told me to wake you up after my guard."

"OK," he replied reluctantly, sitting up and staring into the darkness.

"Can you find your way to the guard position?"

"Sure."

"OK, you wake up Mazz."

"Roger that." Bill grabbed his weapon and hat, which had been carefully placed next to him several hours before. There was no moon. Furthermore, the bamboo blocked any ambient light. Starting out from his hootch, the LT moved rather quickly, for he knew the general location of the guard position. But as he walked, limbs, vines, and trees constantly popped up in front of him, slowing him down and throwing him off course. Much to Bill's frustration and anger he couldn't locate the guard position. He was disoriented. Platoon leaders like to think they are rarely lost but frequently disoriented. Tripping over someone's hootch, Bill had no choice but to get help.

"Wake up, wake up," he said softly, poking someone he could feel but couldn't see.

"Who is it?"

"It's the LT. I can't find the guard position."

Rolling out of his hootch, the grunt put his boots on and walked over to the position with no difficulty.

"Here it is, LT," he whispered, some ten meters from Bill. Not able to see him, the LT moved in the direction of his voice. "Don't bump your head on the poncho." He gave the LT the handset of the radio.

"Thanks," Bill said, pausing momentarily to get a squelch on the radio. "By the way, who is this?"

"Gonzales."

"Oh, I'm sorry I had to get you up, John."

"That's OK, LT," he replied as he headed back to his hootch.

"Oh, hey, where is Mazzatenta sleeping?"

"Two hootches to your right," came the reply.

"Thanks." Bill's guard watch was almost half over as he sat down. Inside he was laughing at himself. Shortly thereafter, with only a few minutes left on his shift, he decided he had better wake up Joe, since it might take a little while to find him. Starting out from the guard position, he moved in what he thought was the general direction. Tripping over a hootch, he bent down, hoping it was Joe's. "Joe, wake up. Time for guard."

"His hootch is on the right," came a faint reply.

"Oh, OK. Thanks." Crashing through more brush and vines, making all kinds of noise, Bill couldn't, for the life of him, find Joe's hootch. Managing to get back to the one he just tripped over, he knelt down to seek help once again.

"Hey, wake up. Wake up, it's the LT."

Moaning slightly, John Burcham sat up, his outline barely visible in the darkness.

"I can't find Mazzatenta's hootch," Bill said reluctantly.

Without a word, John put on his boots and with hardly any effort, made his way over to Joe's position.

"I'm OK, LT," Joe whispered as he approached. "Can you find your way back now?"

"No problem…uh, I don't know who you wake up. I was supposed to have last guard."

"I'll work it out, LT."

Doing an about-face, Bill began his trek back. As befitting a newbie in the bush, it took him another fifteen minutes to reach his hootch. Joe was softly laughing with each step his LT took. Lying down, Bill decided in the morning he would shoot an azimuth to the guard position, as well as pace off the distance. That way he would surely be able to find it should guard shifts get screwed up again. Bill had been used to the last shift, when there was enough morning light to move around easily, when he didn't have to worry about waking anyone else. Needless to say, he made a lot of noise stumbling around the perimeter, not to mention causing at least two men a doubly interrupted night's sleep. Fortunately, for his sake, he didn't wander outside the perimeter. Had he tripped a flare, someone might have blown him away with a claymore mine.

Every evening, just before darkness, the men put out trip flares all around the perimeter. They were placed just beyond the claymores. The flares served as an early warning against enemy approach. Each was normally attached to a tent peg which was placed in the ground. A twenty-five foot wire run from the flare to a tree or other sturdy object was tightened just enough so that something hitting the wire would set off the flare. The policy on guard was to blow a claymore if a flare went off. On occasion the GIs would trip their own, and would immediately yell "friendly," indicating it was an accident and not the enemy. It sure didn't do much for a grunt's nerves, though, when caught on the wrong side of a claymore mine with a flare burning brightly, especially if he knew the guy on guard was quick with that clacker.

The weather continued wet and muggy, often playing havoc with communications, especially during the daylight hours. On several occasions it became a real cause for concern. The Second and Fourth platoons were still operating to the north. But there were instances when the CP did not have commo with them for two or three hours at a time. This was dangerous, for if the platoons became involved in a contact, the CO had no way to coordinate support, often critical to the unit. Even when commo was working, transmissions were sometimes broken and distorted, creating aggravation for all concerned. Setting up in valleys, or any low area for that matter, was just asking for trouble. High ground was not only tactically superior, it also provided the best radio reception.

The night following the LT's fiasco on guard, an incident occurred which was anything but amusing. One member of the mortar crew began having hallucinations while on guard. His screams were heard throughout the perimeter and beyond. The individual locked and loaded his M-16 on one of Bill's men who approached to quiet him down. It was a tense moment, but the grunt did settle down and managed to remain quiet for the rest of the night. In the morning he was sent back to Bien Hoa by medevac for observation. Things were bad enough for the grunts without them having to worry about one of their own making it any worse.

The next morning Bill took out his first long patrol. The CO gave him the mission to search the area surrounding an old abandoned firebase. It was about a klick (one thousand meters) south of the perimeter. After plotting his route with compass and map, he preplanned mortar fire along the intended course. He was taught to always do this before going out on patrol. Normally the preplanned targets were hilltops, stream junctions, and roads. In the event they got in a contact, the mortar crew would have the precise settings for the adjustment point Bill chose. This saved the mortar crew a great deal of time, time that could have made the difference between life and death for the men on patrol.

They moved out in a long file, with Sergeant Houston now walking in the rear. It was slow moving the majority of the way. Vines, fallen trees, and heavy brush made every step an effort. They did reach an open area, however, and Bill stopped short of it to give his men a rest. He also wanted to test the mortar crew.

"Eight-seven, eight-seven, four-five, over."

"Eight-seven, go ahead."

"This is four-five, roger, I'd like you to crank up on alpha two for me."

"Roger, got a solid, wait one." In a few minutes the mortar crew called back. "Four-five, eight-seven, we're ready."

"Eight-seven, four-five, go ahead."

The faint sound of the mortar tube way back in the perimeter could be heard.

"Four-five, eight-seven, you've got a shot."

"Roger, shot."

"Four-five, eight-seven, you've got a splash."

Just at that moment they heard the impact, and shortly thereafter saw the white smoke of the WP round.

"Direction eighteen hundred, range four hundred meters, repeat HE," Bill instructed, pointing his compass in the direction of the smoke and estimating the distance from where he was standing. Directions were given in mils rather than degrees.

"Understand direction eighteen hundred, range four hundred, repeat HE."

"Roger, you've got a solid."

Once again the round came in, only this time it was the high explosive he asked for. The LT adjusted a few more HE rounds, bringing them in closer to his temporary position before calling an end of mission. The mortar crew did a fine job. They had put the rounds exactly where Bill wanted them. The exercise seemed to give his men more confidence in the mortar crew, something they had lacked for a long time.

They reached the abandoned firebase a short while later but found no signs of recent activity in the vicinity. Making their final turn to the north, they headed straight back. About two hundred meters south of the perimeter, however, Bill became disoriented and had to call the CP for help. The CO told Bill to stand by as one of the men in the CP would fire three M-16 rounds. With this help Bill was able to get back on course and they returned to the perimeter a short time later. It was a tiring trip, but one that gave the LT added confidence and experience.

During supper that evening Bill sat with Reynaldo Torres and Joe Greaux along the perimeter. The unusually dark nights became a subject of conversation.

"We had a guy several months ago, LT, who would take a leak on my rucksack every damn night," Torres said. "He couldn't see what the fuck he was doing."

"Can you believe that, LT?" said Joe, turning toward Bill and laughing.

"Yes, I can. Yes, I can," the LT replied, thinking about his somewhat related experience a few nights before. They broke up before it got too dark. Bill made one loop within the perimeter, as was his usual custom, and then hit the sack.

On the ninth day into the mission the other platoons began to report signs of activity. The Fourth Platoon was patrolling about two klicks northeast of the CP. Around one-thirty in the afternoon they spotted someone.

"What have you got?" inquired the CP RTO who took the initial call.

"A gook. We're chasing him," came the excited reply.

"You need Max?" Bill inquired, taking the horn. The CO had gone back to Bien Hoa for a commander's briefing, leaving the LT in charge of the CP.

"Negative," said LT Thorp, taking the handset from his RTO. "Stand by for a sit rep, though."

The CP was not in any immediate danger but Bill alerted his platoon and the mortar crew anyway. When he was finally able to summarize his situation, Wes said they failed to catch the gook but did recover a cache of corn. He also reported a few trails and bunkers in the area.

A sit rep (situation report) had to be called in to the CP whenever a contact occurred, or whenever something tactically significant was encountered. It was then forwarded to battalion. Platoon leaders had to call in descriptions of trails, bunkers, campsites, anything they thought battalion might find useful and informative. This information was the basis for the construction and updating of intelligence reports.

LT Thorp found no need to call for air support this time, but four different types were available had he made the request. A medevac bird (a Huey having the Red Cross symbol painted on the sides) was on call when anyone had to be extracted, whatever the reason. If the bird could land the operation was as simple as placing someone in an ambulance. Since the grunts spent most of their time in the jungle, where LZs were few and far between, the operation was normally more complex. Depending on the nature of the injury, the casualty was either hoisted up through the trees on a jungle penetrator (JP) or in a rigid litter. The JP was used when he had full use of his arms. It was an L-shaped device on which he sat, and was raised and lowered from the bird using an electrical winch and cable. A rigid litter was used otherwise. The casualty was strapped in from head to toe and hoisted up in the same manner as the JP. The whole operation took about five minutes if everything went well. The medevac bird, of course, had to hover directly overhead throughout the whole process.

Then there was Max, the helicopter gunship. Where the name originated no one seemed to really know, but it might have been synonymous with the German air medal of the same name. The loaches, or light observation helicopters, were part of the Red Team (as opposed to Blue Max or the Blue Team). They normally carried just one pilot, along with an observer or gunner. They were used to spot trails, bunkers or anything tactically significant on the ground. Flying at treetop level, they were extremely vulnerable to enemy fire. Often this bird was accompanied by Max and the combination was called the Pink Team. While the gunship could have fired on targets detected by the loach, normally it was just there to provide security, and so circled high above the little bird.

RASH, the forward air controller (FAC), flew a light, fixed wing aircraft, directing jet fighters onto the targets. Coordination of an air strike was between the ground commander and RASH, not with the jet fighter pilots themselves. When RASH came on station he would automatically come up on the company push. The fighters remained on a completely different frequency. Max, RASH, the Pink Team, and the medevac were all available if and when needed. It was certainly comforting to know Charlie didn't have anything of the kind on which to rely.

The next morning, to go along with the excitement of the previous day, a shot from an M-16 broke the dead silence of first light. The men all scrambled for their weapons and cover, until they learned the "gook" turned out to be an animal. These events didn't do much for their nerves, but it did indicate they were alert. In the mid to late sixties American units were involved in contacts almost on a daily basis. When movement was detected, they fired, regardless of whether it was man or animal. The tendency to fire at movement now seemed to have disappeared. Only the real veterans did it. Most of the newbies were inclined to assume it was an animal, and fire only if they actually saw the enemy. There were arguments supporting both sides, but Bill never enforced any particular rule. In his mind, the situation and mental attitude of the people involved would dictate the appropriate action.

One day later brought word of another change in plans. The insignificant findings and the nearness of the political elections in Saigon prompted battalion to move into a completely new AO. This meant that firebase Charles would be closing down, and a new one, Sherman, would provide the new base of operations. The new AO facilitated fast movement to the city should riots develop during the elections. For Alpha Company, specifically, it meant being extracted from the bush back to Charles for a brief stop, and then on to Sherman, stopping there too just long enough to catch their breath, before going back into the bush. The leapfrogging from bush to firebase to bush was necessitated by the closing of Charles. Battalion would be unable to support the grunts with artillery while they were in their current location. In the new AO, though, Alpha Company would be within range of the howitzers on Sherman.

The brief stop at Charles was memorable. When they arrived it was almost completely stripped. Huge crane helicopters were lifting the last few artillery pieces out. Damn if that reddish dirt wasn't blown in everyone's face and hair again. Not long ago the grunts built that base. Now they were tearing it down.

5

Skies grew dark as the men fumbled through the heavy vegetation, trying to get themselves locked in one large NDP. They knew the rain was imminent. It was just a matter of whether they could get their hootches up in time to stay dry. Alpha had made brief stops at Charles and Sherman, and was once again in the triple-canopy jungle, back to the thankless job of endless patrolling.

Why the hell did the CO pick this spot, Bill thought, moving from one position to another, ensuring his men were setting up correctly. They were on high ground but visibility was generally poor. The heavy brush made even the little things extremely difficult. Linking everyone together took ages. Rain began falling hard as the LT finished his task and walked back to the spot where he had dropped his ruck. It pissed him off to be getting soaked and not even started on the construction of his own hootch. All he could think of was how cold it would be that night, trying to sleep in wet clothes. Morning seemed to take forever, but with it came warm sunshine. Ponchos and liners were left out to dry in the sun.

"I'm going out with you today, Bill," the CO said, sipping hot coffee and munching on a pecan cake roll.

The LT ate breakfast with him on occasion, taking the opportunity to discuss their future plans and reflect on past accomplishments. Bill found it difficult to believe they were really helping the Vietnamese. He even doubted the Vietnamese appreciated the presence of GIs in their country. While Captain Silver never succeeded in convincing Bill he was wrong to think that way, just rapping about the subject made the LT feel better. The move from Charles to Sherman reflected a withdrawal of sorts, toward the population centers. Bill never stopped hoping for another move, one that would actually put them within the city limits. Rumors ran rampant all the time. Some even went so far as to say the Cav was about to stand down.

"Where will we be going?" the LT inquired, a huge bite of pound cake muffling his voice.

"We're going to check out the near bank of the Song Be River for sampan landing sites. Let's be ready to move out in thirty minutes."

"Roger that."

Bill tossed the empty pound cake can into the brush and poured out the remainder of his hot chocolate, now almost cold. The sun was very bright, reflecting off large leaves that surrounded them. At midday those same leaves would provide some welcome shade. The LT pulled his map out and studied it before heading back to his hootch.

"Oh, Bill, bring a few trip flares and enough wire to reach across the river. I'm going to see if we can rig up an early warning device on that blue."

"Yes, sir."

The VC and NVA were ingenious when it came to logistics. They found all conceivable means to move equipment past American units. The rivers and waterways of South Vietnam provided one of the best means for doing this, particularly during the hours of darkness. Sampans floated with the current and essentially made no noise whatsoever.

With the men briefed and the required equipment ready, the Third Platoon set out on the light escapade. The CO walked about midway in the file, pretty much letting his LT run the show. Fortunately the terrain opened up near the river, so it wasn't too difficult moving and judging location. In fact, the men left behind in the perimeter could observe the patrol part of the way, peering from a spot on their hilltop home.

The near bank of the river turned out to be extremely steep, providing few if any decent landing sites. The far side was much better, but unfortunately they weren't allowed to work the other bank. Alpha was given two grid squares to work on this mission. It was essential that the men remain within this designated area all the time. Most operations were based on the fact that there were no friendlies in the area. If movement was detected, or an individual seen, it was automatically considered enemy. Had they crossed the river and begun patrolling, they might have encountered another American unit. The encounter could have easily resulted in a friendly firefight.

It was evident almost right away that the CO's plan to trip the river would be impossible. The blue must have been fifty meters wide. The current was so swift even Tarzan wouldn't have been able to swim across. The patrol continued searching the near bank, however, and periodically found a campsite. Each time they found one, Bill called the CO on the horn. He would come up to the front of the file, very interested in the interpretation Bill's men had regarding the site. It was difficult to determine who used the campsites, but the grunts concluded they must have been used by individuals making their way down the river by boat. There were no trails to be seen emerging from the riverbank. Had the CO been able to string a wire across and attach a flare, he might have been lucky and found out just who was traveling on that river.

Paralleling the blue for six hundred meters, the patrol began to make a wide turn and soon headed back to the perimeter. This was the first time the CO had been out with Bill and had nothing but compliments for his men on their return. While they were out, battalion had called to issue afternoon storm warnings. The monsoon season was now at its peak, raining heavily every day as faithfully as "Old Faithful."

Things remained quiet during the night but the following morning was a different story. A few members of the Second Platoon walked out of the perimeter and spotted an anteater. It was just too tempting, and so they proceeded to blow it away with their M-16s. Of course, the men who remained in the perimeter all dove for cover, uncertain what was happening. It seems the group failed to inform everyone of their departure. This was another instance where friendly fire could have easily occurred.

This was log day. But the resupply included more than the usual rations. Colonel Hodges, the new battalion commander, made a visit escorting, to everyone's surprise and delight, two girls from the Red Cross. Bill's new platoon sergeant arrived too. Sergeant Houston was scheduled to return to Bien Hoa on September 8 to begin preparation for his return to the United States on September 15. In the meantime, he wanted to work with his replacement, Sergeant Ramsey, so the transition would be relatively easy for the LT and platoon. The men learned later in the day, unfortunately, that their mission had been extended for three days. They would be moving north along the river, again as a company. What a bitter disappointment, for it meant they would not get back to Sherman in time to see Miss America. She and a small group of entertainers were touring firebases in South Vietnam.

This was just one of many letdowns that affected the men emotionally and mentally. The grunts were fighting in a war far from home and loved ones. Their only contact with life back in the world was through the mail and infrequent visits by VIPs. They would cling to these outlets as their only connection to a sense of home, love, and appreciation. Without some knowledge of recognition for their work and efforts, they soon became discouraged. News from home and friends always made their job seem a little more bearable. But when the letters and visitors didn't come, it seemed to make things twice as bad.

Bill became emotionally involved with a girl from Georgia before his arrival in Vietnam. She told him she would write during his tour. But after three unanswered letters, the LT really began to feel discouraged. She had meant a lot to him at the time, and still did, but when he needed her comforting thoughts and cheerful humor it wasn't there. He always received letters from his parents, relatives, and friends, but somehow this loss hurt him. For a while he didn't know what to do. Putting things in perspective, though, he realized it was more important to having loving parents and the close camaraderie he shared with his men. Time was a wonderful healer too.

You know, Bill later thought, I'll bet the colonel brought those doughnut dollies out here as a substitute for the show he knew the grunts would miss. I really admire his thoughtfulness. He didn't have to do that.

Alpha Company awoke the next morning wet from the night's rain. The move began about eight o'clock but was halted soon thereafter when one of the men in the Second Platoon suffered a leg injury. He had to be medevaced. The CO switched the order of movement when the trek began again. It was now Fourth Platoon, CP, mortar, third, and second. With yesterday's resupply, rucksacks bulged and felt like a ton. Movement was slow and very difficult. The company crossed a major blue and stopped well beyond the far bank for lunch. Bill's platoon took over the lead thereafter. Alpha reached its planned NDP site with about three hours of daylight remaining. Everyone was exhausted. The leeches had been very bad all along the way. When the rain began falling in the early evening it brought the mosquitoes out too. Bill actually welcomed the rain this time for he was down to his last canteen of water. It didn't take long to fill the empties with rainwater flowing off his poncho. Artillery rounds to the east and west were heard throughout the night.

The following morning Bill took a patrol six hundred meters north but found nothing. LT Thorp also had negative results searching to the west. Polling his men after returning to the perimeter, Bill found their major complaint to be a lack of information as to what was going on. The LT recalled experiencing the same feeling in OCS when he was on patrol in Georgia and not in a leadership position. Somewhere in the chain of command communication was breaking down. The LT suspected his squad leaders were not taking enough time to brief their men.

While the day proved to be uneventful and time went by slowly, it did give the men a chance to relax somewhat. It was August 28, one year ago to the day that Bill graduated from OCS. That was merely a passing thought for him, though. Having responsibility for the lives of seventeen individuals seemed to dominate all his thinking.

Extraction day finally arrived and all eagerly packed their equipment. It had been a long, tiring mission, even though signs of enemy activity were not found. For some unknown reason, however, battalion placed Alpha on alert as a ready reaction force. The men didn't think they'd get back to the firebase as planned. Morale reached an all time low at this point.

"Damn, not again!" Bill said to himself upon hearing the news. "What the hell is this?"

A ready reaction force (RRF) was often employed when an aircraft went down and security during rescue was needed. It was also employed when a unit in contact needed reinforcements. Generally the RRF was drawn from one or more units already on the firebase. But sometimes battalion just extended the mission of a unit scheduled to come in from the bush.

Soon word came down that Alpha was released from this status and would proceed to Sherman as originally planned. The extraction went smoothly. Before long the grunts were on the firebase, relaxing in a bright, hot sun with a beer in one hand and mail from home in the other. There would be plenty of details for the next few days, but in the meantime the guys just relaxed. Letters from home brought news of friends and loved ones. Relief and satisfaction permeated Bill's mind. He had just completed his first mission as a platoon leader.

There were a number of regulations that had to be observed while on the firebase. One pertained to beards. Simply stated, they weren't allowed. Bill hardly recognized his men after they all cleaned up. For some it was a major task just shaving off a fifteen-day growth. One of the big pluses about the firebase, though, was the Mess Daddy. He lived and worked for the GIs, drawing as much respect and admiration as did the battalion commander. It was certainly a welcome change from the bland C-rations the men lived on in the bush. Through the hard work of the grunts, Sherman was being improved continuously. An eight-hour day filling sandbags, building hootches, patrolling, and clearing fields of fire, not to mention the usual trash pickups and shit burning, made for a tired bunch of guys as the sun set. To make matters worse, they had to pull the nightly guard duty, just as in the bush.

While work was always being done, there was time for fun too. A Frisbee was always seen floating around the perimeter. Usually a football or basketball game would develop. Somehow the grunts had excess energy to burn. By far the most popular game among the grunts was card playing. It was unbelievable how much money changed hands in these games. Bill never allowed his men to play while on a mission because he felt they would forget about security. In his mind, card playing implied a relaxed, passive, often jovial atmosphere. The bush was certainly nothing of the kind. He did allow them to read during a mission, however. This was because their security never dropped as they read. Ears were still perked to hear the slightest noise from outside the perimeter.

It was a bright, sunny afternoon. Bill sat on the top of his hootch cleaning his weapon and ammunition. The M-16 was dependable, and perfect for the environment in which they were fighting. When it became too dirty, however, the M-16 could jam, especially if the ammo was also dirty. Ammunition carried on a mission was normally fired up once the grunts got back to the firebase. A new supply was drawn before the next mission. When they couldn't fire it up, though, it had to be cleaned.

"Hey, Bill, let's play some basketball," the CO said as he came over to see what Bill was doing.

"Sure," Bill replied and promptly put his work aside. He never refused an offer to play basketball, even if it was in Vietnam. The officers walked over to a crude court on the outside of the bourn, borrowing a ball from the medics. The day was extremely hot. Smoke from burning shit was blowing right in their faces. In a short while they had a game going. Bill and the CO were pitted against two staff sergeants. It turned out to be a very clumsy game, with the LT resting periodically due to smoke inhalation and exhaustion. But the officers were able to squeak out a win, much to their enjoyment.

The firebase provided a chance for the men to relax mentally too. There was plenty of opportunity to write letters or just dream endless dreams. Often Bill stared up at the stars at night, trying to picture what his relatives and friends back in the world were doing at that very moment. Thoughts of his parents, sisters, and that girl from Georgia were dominant. He couldn't help but reflect on their mission just passed also. Sometimes the thought of being a platoon leader in Vietnam seemed exciting and rewarding to him. Other times, just the very thought of being so far from home, with the uncertainty of their future, actually made him hate and fear the country, the war and the army. Even though Bill now had confidence in himself and his men, he was very apprehensive about their upcoming missions. It was difficult living moment by moment. But then one never knew if one would live to see the next day, so it became just another routine, not a matter of choice.

The company held an awards ceremony on Sherman before dark on the last day of their stay. The colonel presented numerous awards for meritorious action, several to Bill's men for contacts of which he was unaware, contacts that had taken place a month before his arrival in country. Bill also stood in the line of awardees. The colonel wanted to pin a first lieutenant's bar on his fatigue shirt. Rain began falling as the battalion commander made his last few remarks. It was a little unusual to see the men in formation, with their dirty uniforms, tarnished boots and ragged steel pots. But it made the LT feel good to know they were getting some recognition for their difficult job. Bill was unaware that when an LT gets promoted he buys drinks for his men. A few were quick to inform him of that custom, however. He ended up having to buy beers for his whole platoon, the CO, and a few other pertinent individuals. The party had to break up early, though, for the rain began to fall very hard.

The next morning sixteen new replacements from the rear reported to Captain Silver. He divided them up pretty evenly among his three platoons. Bill's lance (number of men in the field) increased to twenty-two. He actually had twenty-nine men assigned, but seven were either in Bien Hoa or on R&R. The company was beginning to get its strength back. Of course, more men meant added responsibility. Bill was very cognizant of this fact as he briefed his new men on the upcoming missions.

6

The time at Sherman was short-lived, just as it was at Charles. Once again the battalion was moving into an entirely new AO. Little time was wasted planning the move. All useable equipment and building materials were removed from Sherman by Chinook. The bourn and most bunkers inside were left intact, to be leveled later by bulldozers. Sherman had been a big improvement over Charles, with its hardtop helicopter pads and steel hooches, the latter carefully constructed so dirt didn't continually filter through the walls. The men hoped the same would be true of Mace, the name given to their new firebase. As it turned out, little construction work had to be done at Mace. Another battalion had been using the firebase prior to the arrival of the First of the Seventh. They would now share it. Basically all that was needed were additional living quarters and a few supplementary positions. Vietnamese women were employed to help with kitchen work, so that was one less job for the grunts to do.

When the last Chinook sortie left Sherman so did the company, and they began calling Mace their home. Not long after Alpha's arrival it was learned there would be two more

Chinook sorties required to transfer all the useable equipment. These last two loads were timber and concertina wire located at Charles. Bill didn't know whether it was by choice or chance, but his platoon was given the mission to secure the area while the logistics people completed the transfer. Why the hell do they still have equipment at Charles, the LT pondered. God, it was abandoned three weeks ago.

The only intelligence received about the area was that a Ranger team had killed two VC inside the bourn approximately one week prior. The bodies were just left there. Bill's main concern about this mission was the possibility of hitting booby traps. While they presented more of a problem to American units operating in the north, it was not uncommon for the VC and NVA in Alpha's AO to employ them too. For this reason Bill wanted to be extremely cautious. In fact, he planned on not walking inside the bourn regardless of where the salvageable material was located. The logistics people could do that.

Since the VC were scavengers, the grunts always expected Charlie to come snooping around a firebase once it was abandoned. A Ranger team was sometimes left behind, positioned within the abandoned base, to ambush any inquisitive visitors. The team normally consisted of five or six men. Although they were few in number, they built elaborate ambushes all around their position utilizing claymore mines. Some of these mines were set up to be command detonated, while others were automated with a battery attachment and trip wire. The team had commo with battalion at all times and so could request air support if it was necessary. Ranger teams were in the bush no more than a week at a time. They were extracted immediately upon recording a step-on (kill). This normally meant three days off before having to go out again. The two dead VC attested to the success of the Ranger team this time. It was obvious the bodies were intentionally left there to make others think twice about stepping foot on the old base.

Yellow One arrived shortly after eleven o'clock and carried the Third Platoon to the abandoned base. When they hit the ground, the CO who accompanied them directed Bill to sweep across the firebase, much to the LT's dissatisfaction. The CO was more concerned about the possibility of VC holed up in the bunkers than hitting booby traps. In any event, Bill had no choice but to sweep across. This is almost like a scene from a movie, he thought, as his men moved from one bunker to another, ensuring each was clear of personnel and equipment. The task was as dangerous as it was difficult. Each bunker was pitch dark inside. Many were partially caved in. The men could have easily talked themselves out of having to enter them. But the job had to be done. Colonel Hodges, flying overhead, requested permission to land. Bill received the call but told him to wait until the entire area was secure. In about fifteen minutes they completed the search and secured the old firebase. Hodges landed several minutes later and joined the CO and LT within the bourn. Bill had been so absorbed in the sweep of the base, he completely forgot about the equipment that was to be hooked out.

"Position your men around the timber and wire, Bill." the CO said, pointing over the bourn toward the northwest. At that same moment the smell of decaying bodies hit Bill. He instantly remembered the report of those two VC who were left unburied near the TOC. The platoon had covered the entire firebase but the LT personally bypassed the TOC.

"Boy, what a smell," he said to Captain Silver, as he stepped up onto the bourn, facing in the direction the CO had indicated. He now could see how the material was laid out. "OK, sir, I'll move my men in position right away."

It took more time than the CO preferred, but the LT finally got his people in place. With all-around security attained, they had only to wait on the Chinooks. Bill sat down near a supplementary position in the bourn and opened up a can of peanut butter and crackers, one of his staples. The smell of the decaying bodies was inescapable, for the grunts were downwind of them. Although he certainly could have done without it, this was the first opportunity Bill had to see, up close, the horrible effects of war. The VC were lying at the entrance to the TOC. Their bodies were bloated and covered with maggots. Considering they were hit by claymores at close range, it was amazing the bodies were even intact.

The LT gazed around the firebase, trying to picture where things were located when the base was active. It looked so different now. Orienting on the partially destroyed TOC, he traced the route he had walked almost one month before, when he came out here to meet his battalion commander. How rapidly things change. They had moved from two different firebases, seen one battalion commander leave and another take his place. There had been a continual turnover of their own men too. Sergeant Houston was gone. He left for DEROS, completing his third and final tour of Vietnam. There were actually men in Bill's platoon now with less time in country than he had. The question in the LT's mind was whether these changes reflected a hope for something better. Maybe their luck would run out instead. So much of what they did, so much of what occurred was really just a matter of chance, fate, luck, whatever you wanted to call it. In some sense it seemed they were playing a game of Russian roulette. But then, Charlie was in the same game.

It was a sunny, hot day. The grunts had to just sit and wait, with no shade to give them relief. Bill's mind wandered. He contemplated how dreadful it would be if they were left here, and had to spend the night. He wondered too what it would be like to climb down into one of those bunkers, alone, with nobody else around, and then, all of a sudden, hear the sound of VC coming over the bourn from the wood line. A chill ran down his spine, but his daydreaming ended when that awful smell filled the air once again.

"What's the story with the shithooks?" Bill inquired of the pathfinder, sitting up above him on top of a bunker.

"Don't know, LT" he replied, squinting into the sun, his face dotted with droplets of sweat.

Pathfinders were specifically trained in ground-to-air communications. On a firebase, their responsibility was identification of aircraft approaching the base. They transmitted instructions to each pilot, depending, of course, on the specific mission. Chinooks carrying supplies to the base had to be directed to the proper drop zone. Items to be picked up had to be clearly identified. The pathfinder helped to accomplish all of this through his radio contact with the pilots and use of smoke grenades. Most of the cargo carried by a Chinook was transported under its belly, not inside the aircraft. If a sortie called for the pickup of empty water blivots, the equipment would be waiting on the log pad, all strapped together. A "hook man" was waiting on the pad, ready to attach the straps to the Chinook as it settled over the blivots. As the Chinook approached the base, colored smoke would be popped next to these blivots. The pathfinder would tell the pilot to proceed to the colored smoke, thus ensuring that the proper equipment was picked up. He was really an air traffic controller, for on any given day there were many sorties to and from the firebase, each with a specific mission, each trying to minimize blade time. This was accomplished in part by eliminating confusion and error.

Bill had to take a leak. He got up and walked over to a 155 canister placed in the bourn for just such a purpose. Returning to their small perimeter, he felt tired and restless at the same time. The smell of the bodies never seemed to let up. It began to make him sick.

Why the hell didn't they bury them, he thought, gazing from a distance at the lifeless forms rotting in the heat. But this is war, his conscience retorted. The sight and sense of death is all part of this horrible conflict. Get used to it! You're in Vietnam. Didn't they tell you what it was like over here?

> You see the napalm burning, those it killed and maimed,
> You pray that you won't get the same.

Off in the distance he could see a Chinook headed their way. Could this be ours, he thought, as he hurried over to the bunker where the pathfinder was perched.

"Yeah, this is one of them, LT," he said, as Bill approached.

"All right!" the LT responded happily.

"The other should be right behind."

"Sure hope so. I'm anxious to leave this place."

Shortly thereafter purple smoke was popped for the pilots. By two o'clock all the material was hooked out. The platoon moved to the deserted CA pad when word came that Yellow One was inbound.

"They're not wasting any time," Bill said to his platoon sergeant, as they both made ready to depart.

"Yeah, and I don't mind one bit either," the sergeant replied.

The men split up into the usual groups of five and climbed aboard the birds as they touched down. In a moment the grunts were carried high above the trees. Rounds from their M-16s and the M-60s mounted on the slicks ripped through the dense jungle below, covering their extraction. As the clear, fresh air blew hard against his face and dangling legs, the LT felt a sense of relief knowing they had accomplished their mission and were now all safe aboard the helicopters. Charles disappeared from view but Bill doubted it would ever disappear from his mind.

Tomorrow they would be going to Vung Tau. The city would be a welcome break from the bush. It would give the men a chance to get their minds off the war, even if it was for only three days.

7

The stars covered the night sky, forecasting a nice day ahead for the trip to Vung Tau. Alpha was scheduled to leave Mace at eight o'clock. This was one occasion when the men really wanted their transportation to arrive on time. Bill had never been to Vung Tau, but the early morning conversation about the girls, the Palace Hotel, and the beach was getting him excited. He was really looking forward to the next three days. With breakfast over, the men checked to make sure their rucksacks contained the usual combat equipment. Even though they were standing down temporarily, they had to be prepared for any emergency. No city, hamlet, or village in Vietnam was considered truly safe. The VC were known to strike when you least expected it.

At seven forty-five a truck pulled up in front of the billets. Bill packed his platoon on for the short ride to the Chinook pad. Morale was high as the men piled onto the truck. Arms, legs, weapons and rucksacks were all jammed together in a huge mess. Five minutes later they arrived at the hook pad and had to disentangle themselves to get off the truck. The LT had been given a few pointers from the CO earlier and wanted to relay this information to his men.

"Get the men in a group, Sarge, so I can talk to them," he told his platoon sergeant. The men quickly gathered, laughing and talking about the resort city as they moved closer together.

"OK, listen up," Bill shouted, waiting for a few stragglers to join the group. "For those of you who have never been to Vung Tau, and that includes myself, we're told there are a few things to watch out for. We'll be going to Xuan Loc first. Be careful of the Vietnamese people there. They'll be waiting at the airfield to sell you cokes, hats, and all sorts of things. Remember not to give them MPC. The cashier at the R&R center will convert it to piasters. And don't get into a fight with them, OK? The best thing to do is ignore them."

"LT, what if we already have piasters?" one of Bill's men inquired.

"Then you're all set. That's the currency you'll use. Listen, I'm not implying I want you to refrain from buying anything. Just don't hassle them. You know what I mean."

"Yeah, we know," Bill Talbott replied

"Another thing," the LT said. "It shouldn't cost you more than forty for the trip downtown."

"There's also a free bus, LT," Talbott added.

"Oh, OK. Did you guys hear that? Talbott says there's free bus service."

When the GIs arrived in Vietnam all their greenbacks were converted to military payment certificates (MPC). This currency was used to purchase goods and services on American bases overseas. In order to make purchases on the Vietnamese market, the MPC had to be converted to piasters, the basic currency of Vietnam. While the MPC dollar was equivalent to the greenback dollar, it was worth about four hundred piasters on the Vietnamese exchange. Since Vietnam's economy was nowhere near as strong as the U.S. economy, the grunts could purchase clothes, stereo equipment, cameras, and many food items for a fraction of what it would cost back in the world.

"You forgot to mention claymores, LT" Sergeant Ramsey said.

"Oh, thanks, Sarge," the LT said, turning back toward his group of men. "Also, listen up," he commanded. The men had started to laugh and talk again. "If you haven't done so already, turn in your claymore mines before departing." The LT paused. "Did you hear me? Turn in all claymores before we leave." Bill stepped aside and motioned for Sergeant Ramsey to add anything.

"In Vung Tau it's best to walk with a buddy," the Sarge began. "Should something happen, at least you'll have help. I strongly recommend this, especially if this is your first trip down there." "Lastly, he shouted, once the briefing at the R&R center is over, you're free, and I don't want to see you until the morning of the fourth day. Have a good time."

"All right!" the noisy, rowdy bunch yelled in unison. They slowly broke up into smaller groups, waiting impatiently for the hooks to arrive.

It was 8:00 a.m. now. The road leading to Mace was active with motor vehicles and Vietnamese on foot, all beginning another workday at the firebase or on neighboring farms. The sky was a deep blue and cloudless. Bill hoped the same would be true at Vung Tau. The whole company had, by this time, reached the pad. All were anxious to leave.

The first hook came in about eight thirty. The platoon loaded aboard. All but their LT, that is. Bill got left behind due to a lack of space. Xuan Loc was only ten minutes away. As the second hook touched down at the airfield, the LT could see his platoon and what appeared to be fifteen or twenty Vietnamese. Among the Vietnamese were little kids and older women. The kids were really cute, with their butch haircuts, inquisitive expressions, and inexhaustible energy. Across the airfield a small Vietnamese firebase made its presence known as a volley of 105s drowned out the voices of the vendors.

"You buy Coke?" a little girl asked softly as she approached the LT.

"No, no thanks," he replied just as softly, watching her eyes travel from his head to toe. At six feet three inches, he must have looked like a giant standing there. His rucksack and weapon were at his feet. In a minute he had at least ten little kids around him, all hoping he was going to buy their Coke, beer, bread, and ice cream. A little boy selling Coke saw that Bill wasn't buying. But he came over as the others left, to see if he could persuade the LT anyway. He put his bare feet on the LT's boots and held out his hands, as if he wanted Bill to dance with him. Actually, his objective was to escape the hot surface of the airfield, for the sun was now overhead and heating up the early morning rapidly. The boy wrapped his arms around the LT's legs. Bill began to walk, taking large steps, much to the boy's enjoyment. The LT was enjoying the whole thing himself.

The older women were content to just sit and watch their small children do their selling. Once in a while, though, they too would approach the grunts. Bill felt sorry for them. Their tired, depressed and sad faces described very well their situation. Some GIs said this was the kind of life they had always known. So maybe Bill shouldn't have felt that way. Knowing no other lifestyle, maybe they were content and happy deep inside. This seemed doubtful to Bill, though, if for no other reason than the fact that the war had separated their families. In most instances, the fathers were fighting in the army along with their older sons. Somewhere too Bill had heard that the ones to suffer most from any war were the civilians. From his initial contact with the people of South Vietnam, this statement seemed to hold a great deal of truth.

Stretching out on the ground, the LT was content to watch the women and children. Out of the corner of his eye he could see a little boy staring at his rucksack. Bill didn't realize it at the time, but the boy was very interested in the two LRRP bags that hung from a D ring. They were left over from the last mission. Bill hadn't bothered to take them off. The little boy sure knew what they were, though, and was probably planning a means to obtain them. He ran out of time, however, for it wasn't long before the first of three fixed wing aircraft touched down, to take the men the rest of the way.

The flight took them right down to the airfield at Vung Tau, headquarters of the Australian Army serving in Vietnam. Popular resort beaches could be seen as the plane banked to make its final approach. Having made a smooth landing, the plane taxied up to a small terminal. A representative from the R&R center met the men and explained what had to be done next. Loading their rucksacks onto a truck, the men boarded a bus which drove them through town to the R&R center, located right on the beach. The bus ride was very interesting because it gave Bill the opportunity to see a

Vietnamese city for the first time. The streets were all paved but very narrow. Lambrettas, Hondas, compact cars and pedestrians all made travel slow and painstaking for the Vietnamese bus driver. Small food and drink stands dotted the route. The laughter and voices from a school playground reminded the LT of his own school days back in the world. Shops and homes were built very close to the road. Often the opened front door provided an opportunity to see, at a glance, the interior of these buildings. The Vietnamese liked bright colors. Their tastes were evident from the colors and designs they chose for their establishments. Dress, however, was conservative. Little change could be noted from one individual to another. Men wore predominantly white shirts and dark pants or shorts. The women always wore long dresses, or more commonly, black slacks or pajamas. Women never showed any portion of their legs. Sandals, slippers and bare feet were common. Only the ARVN soldiers seemed to be wearing boots.

Modified Lambrettas, Vietnam's answer to New York taxi cabs, darted in and out as the bus slowly made its way to the R&R center. Often the three-wheeled vehicles carried as many as ten people, all jammed in like sardines. Actually, the best way to describe them was to imagine a rectangular cab built on the back of a motor scooter, with a second wheel in the rear for stability. Despite their size and design, though, they were rugged vehicles, extremely mobile and economical. The taxi fare was not set as it is in the States. Instead, you had to bargain with the driver. Generally, only when the fare was agreed upon would he take you. The grunts who had been to Vung Tau before normally just got in and told the driver where they wanted to go. Upon arriving at their destination, they would give him what they thought was reasonable. This was usually less than what the driver expected, making him very angry. The men would just smile and walk away, pretending they didn't understand what he was saying.

The sight of white sand and blue water assured the men of Alpha Company of their arrival at the center. They departed the bus and walked a short distance to the briefing area, squinting in the hot sun that reflected off the sand. The men didn't have the luxury of sunglasses, portable radios, and coolers. Instead, they carried an M-16, a rucksack, and plenty of excess energy.

Following a short briefing, which explained the regulations with which they had to comply, the men picked up their passes and were free to do as they pleased. Hot showers and all the food they could eat, three times a day, were available at the center. But the men were not too interested in these things. Downtown were available air-conditioned hotel rooms, bars, and most importantly, girls to satisfy their every need. For some of the married men in Alpha Company, the thought of sleeping with a Vietnamese girl presented problems. They found it difficult to decide between the moral marriage oath they took and the physical desire they felt at the moment. A tough decision it was. Some GIs not only slept with girls, after several trips to Vung Tau, they saw the same one each time, and actually became emotionally involved with her. It was very easy for this to happen. Females in Vietnam, as well as in other parts of Asia, lived to serve their men. For some of the GIs this was truly a unique experience. The U.S. Army discouraged GI-Vietnamese marriages, though, by making the red tape extremely lengthy and complex.

On the beach, GIs in cutoff fatigues were lying on the white sand, absorbing the warm rays of the sun. Others were challenging the surf with their bodies. A few even tested their skills on boards provided free by the R&R center. Mingling with the GIs were Vietnamese people dressed in the more familiar bikinis and trunks.

Boy, this is great, Bill thought, walking along the beach, having taken a long, hot shower beforehand. The sand burned the bottoms of his feet. The glare from the sun made things almost too bright to see. Working at the R&R center, or in downtown Vung Tau, would be unbelievable, he surmised. Hell, the people here don't even know there's a war going on! Sitting on a log, he gazed out across the water to land farther southeast. Hills dominated the area, providing a picturesque scene. Toward the northeast, similar hills bordered the city, with mansions built on the summits. Their red-orange roofs were visible for miles. A large, rusty tanker, run aground months earlier, was an unusual sight silhouetted against the flat, rocky shore at the base of one of these hills. Not too far away from where he was sitting, Bill could hear beer cans popping and steaks sizzling, this amid the voices of a group of GI picnickers. They were enjoying a warm and friendly barbeque right on the beach. There were other GIs here besides Alpha Company, all enjoying the short vacation experience. Walking back to the R&R center a short while later, Bill decided to have supper.

"You're not downtown yet, LT?" one of his men asked as Bill approached.

"No, not yet, but I'll be there shortly," he replied, laughing.

Following supper in the mess hall, where he stuffed himself with all sorts of foods from the buffet, he walked to the bus stop to catch that free lift downtown. It was noticeably cooler now. The sun appeared reddish as it got lower in the sky. The bus stopped at the Palace Hotel, the place he had heard so much about. Stepping out, three or four Vietnamese women and children immediately surrounded him, producing briefcases of souvenirs and other wares. They acted like he should buy them out.

"GI buy watch?" one kept asking. Others held up rings and necklaces, saying nothing, just hoping for a sale.

"Not now," he replied, trying to move to the Palace entrance.

"GI numba ten," he heard another say as he passed through modern glass doors into a lobby that was as elaborate as any Hilton in the United States. The standard of living in Vietnam is extremely low relative to America. Through the long association with GIs in cities like Vung Tau, however, the city people have gained some notion of U.S. living standards and material desires. They have managed to capitalize on the exorbitant tastes of the GIs. They were truly high-pressure salesmen of all conceivable goods and services. Familiar with military rank, they knew officers had more money than the average enlisted man. If you purchased something from them you were "numba one" in their mind. But if you didn't buy from them, all the politeness in the world wouldn't help. They loudly called you a "numba ten," letting everyone nearby know just what they thought of you.

On the mezzanine, a restaurant and Playboy bar catered to guests and visitors. Bill hadn't been briefed about Saigon tea and so was totally ignorant of its significance as he ventured into the bar. The entrance was blocked by Vietnamese girls in miniskirts and rather revealing blouses. He walked straight ahead into a dimly lit room. The bar itself was located on one side, with cramped booths on the other. A girl immediately grabbed his hand and led him to a table. He could see other GIs now, as his night vision became a little better. As she sat down, a drink was placed in front of her. A Vietnamese waiter asked in broken English, what the LT wished to drink. Bill ordered a Coke and paid six hundred piasters, about two dollars, for their drinks. The girl remained silent for a few minutes, just gazing into his eyes. Finally, speaking fairly good English, she asked his name and where he was from in America. They talked for a while about the war, his job (he told her he worked in the jungle), and life in a Vietnamese city. The waiter looked over periodically to check on them. The girl had come from Saigon where she had worked in a dress shop. Realizing how much more money she could make as a bar girl and prostitute, she, like many girls, moved to Vung Tau to cater to the needs of the GIs. She told Bill her parents and sister were still in Saigon but that her brother was in the army. She had not heard from him in a long time and didn't know where he was. There were probably hundreds of girls who could have truthfully told the same story.

After buying her three Saigon teas, Bill felt he had had enough. Telling her he would return the next day, he left to see more of the city. Night had fallen as he stepped out onto the street. It was crowded now too with GIs, girls, and motor traffic. The souvenir salesmen were still there. The LT had to discourage them again, for they were persistent in their efforts.

"Me number ten cheap Charlie," he said, smiling at their bright, alert, almost happy faces. He slowly made his way down the sidewalk.

On the other side of the street there was formed literally a wall of bars. Each had a Western-derived name. There was the Texan, Garbo, Hollywood, and Mexican. All served beer and hard liquor, as well as the services of attractive girls. The girls spoke a crude but understandable English, presumably developed over the long association with GIs who came down here on a regular basis. Bright colored signs and lights decorated the entrances to these bars. All of this blended together against the clear night sky to create an almost psychedelic corridor down which Bill walked. Old men and women sat right on the curbs, their movement and gestures seemingly in slow motion, probably reflecting their age and emotion. ARVN soldiers, called cowboys, walked by occasionally. They never really showed an open friendship toward the GIs, though. Lambrettas whizzed by continually, carrying the grunts to all sorts of fun and frolic. Some of the men were not altogether conscious of their destination, but they really didn't care anyway.

"Hey, LT," one guy from his platoon yelled, leaning out of the rear of one of these vehicles. He had a beer in one hand and his girl in the other. Bill waved and smiled. In the bush this guy was a rather quiet but dedicated point man. At this moment, though, he was half bombed out of his mind and enjoying every minute of it.

For once he can really enjoy himself, Bill thought, without the fear of the enemy or the hassle he sometimes gets from me.

The sound of rock music in the hotels had begun to permeate the steady din of voices and traffic. The LT was drawn to one hotel where the band was playing some hit American rock. Although their English was not the best, they sounded great to Bill and he went inside to listen. The interior was not as fashionable as the Palace, but that didn't concern him. Sitting down near the entrance, he was almost immediately joined by a girl in a dark miniskirt. She had long, dark hair, that reached down below her waist. Taking his hand, she was anxious for him to make advances. But the LT's mind was completely absorbed in the music. He hardly realized she was there. She soon left, hoping to find a more sociable companion. Bill methodically waved aside the waiters who approached like clockwork. He was content to just take in the bright, colored lights and the alternating loud and soft music, which filled the smoky, crowded room. The band knew just what songs the GIs liked. The most popular were "I Want To Go Home," "Take Me Home, Country Roads," and "Show Me the Way To Go Home."

Curfew was eleven o'clock. It wasn't until an older American gentleman tapped Bill on the shoulder, telling him he'd better leave or face the MPs, did he realize it was almost eleven thirty. He quickly left the bar and flagged down a Lambretta. It brought him to the Grand Hotel. He had to spend the night there because a room at the Palace was unavailable. As he laid down on a real bed, in the air-conditioned room, his mind replayed everything he'd seen and done that day. Before he knew it morning had arrived.

God, it's only seven o'clock, he said to himself as he glanced at a clock on the wall. Hell, I might as well get up, I'm not tired. The routine of the bush must still be driving me. Having decided to grab breakfast at the R&R center, he quickly got dressed and left the hotel. It felt very warm outside despite the early morning hour. He concluded the air conditioner must be the reason for that. Hopping into another Lambretta, he told the driver R&R center and was whisked away. They passed the open-air market, which was already crowded with weekend shoppers. The smell of fresh bread, fish, and other foods filled the air along the whole market district. Peddlers of all conceivable Oriental food jammed the sidewalks. Bill was surprised to see as many GIs up and around as he did, considering the condition some of them were in the night before. Just think, two more days and nights of this, he thought happily.

It didn't take long to reach the R&R center. Bill gave the driver forty piasters and he seemed very pleased. He drove off and joined the others of his profession along the roadway leading to the center, to wait for his next fare. Bill spent the day on the beach, bodysurfing and getting some sun. That night he returned to the town. He walked around for an hour or so to see as much as he could. Returning to the Playboy bar later in the evening, he met the same girl again. They talked at length about the various customs of the two nations. Vietnamese girls were not supposed to be seen with GIs. Public display of affection was frowned upon. The girls weren't even supposed to ride in the same vehicle with the GIs. When they left the bar they were usually wearing slacks of some kind. This was because the dresses they wore in the bars were very much disrespected in public. In fact, girls were subject to arrest if they were caught on the streets in their "work" outfits.

In a city like Vung Tau it was necessary to control VD. The girls were examined every week. They carried medical cards that indicated when they were last examined. If a GI was in doubt, he was wise to ask the girl for her card. This normally ensured a trouble-free physical relationship. Some of the girls didn't carry cards. The GIs were then in a position of deciding whether they wanted to play the game of Russian roulette.

Bill and his girlfriend had a very interesting conversation that evening. Unbelievably, it cost the LT only one Saigon tea.

The time at Vung Tau passed all too quickly. On the morning of the fourth day the men reluctantly, but responsibly, returned to the R&R center. They now had to retrace their steps back to the firebase. Some were slightly hungover from their drinking. All were noticeably tired, for they understandably packed a week's worth of fun into three short days. Hardly a word was spoken as they slowly pulled their rucksacks and weapons from the connex containers which held them during the stand down. They grouped themselves by platoon for a final count. The CO wanted to be sure no one was left behind. Of course, the grunts wanted to spend the rest of their tour here, but knew that was just wishful thinking. Another company was scheduled to arrive in the early afternoon, just as Alpha did four days earlier. It was a never-ending cycle. Loading onto the bus, Bill couldn't help but recap what he'd seen and done. Only now did he realize why the men looked forward so much to those precious days of fun and sun.

What would the men do, he thought, if they didn't have this outlet as a way to unleash some of their physical and emotional drives? Somebody was really on the ball when he worked out this program.

The bus passed back through the downtown streets. This time it carried a much more reserved group of men. It was now time to start thinking about the next mission and to plan accordingly. Carrying their weapons in hand and rucksacks slung over their shoulders, they were back to reality. It was, once again, forty-five days to Vung Tau.

8

The company didn't get back to Mace until late, and this left them little time to make ready for the CA the following morning. Darkness halted what little they could do that evening. It would be a hectic morning to be sure.

As the sun rose, so did the pace of activity. Morale was low, tempers were short, but somehow they managed to complete the preparations, and had only to wait on Yellow One. Bill attributed the efficient, methodical approach toward the new mission to unbelievably dedicated and conscientious squad leaders.

With the manifest relayed to all concerned, the men leaned back on their packs, easing the weight off their shoulders. Talk was of the past three days, and how hung over some said they still felt.

The mission was to search for enemy activity. Movement would be generally east-northeast once on the ground. They were targeted against the Third Battalion, Thirty-third NVA, a well-equipped and trained force. No one really understood what the overall mission of this enemy unit was, primarily because few documents captured made reference to it. Even when they did, they raised more questions about the elusive, seemingly disorganized force than they answered.

The overall mission of the First of the Seventh Cavalry was to keep the enemy, regardless of the unit, continually on the move. By doing this, it was thought, the gooks would never have a chance to establish any influence on the Vietnamese people. It was believed the main tactic of the VC and NVA was one of forced persuasion, the ultimate objective being to win over the sentiments of the people one way or another. The concept of Vietnamization was completely counter to this. The grunts, in essence, were supporting or aiding the Vietnamization program through their active, offensive patrolling. They were following the basic premise that the best defense is a good offense.

It was difficult for the grunt to view his job in this way because he was faced with the daily job of trying to stay alive. It was only through reflection, when separated from the actual fighting for a period of time, could he somehow justify the effort. But even then, that reflection was rather dim, for pessimistic reports on the progress of Vietnamization were the rule, not the exception. This cast serious doubt in Bill's mind, as to the merits of the program. It seemed the effort was really a lost cause, a misdirected and totally misunderstood concept of what the United States really should have been doing. Going one step further, the question of whether America should have been involved at all also deserved serious study.

Lift push, grid of insertion, and call signs filled the LT's mind as he made last-minute checks with his platoon sergeant and squad leaders. He wanted to ensure they knew what to do once they hit the ground. All too often the grunts were ignorant of what the company's specific mission was, and more importantly, why. Bill tried to make sure they stayed informed by pressuring his E-5s to brief them often.

It was shortly after nine o'clock when notice was given that Yellow One was inbound. The men grimaced as they got to their feet, for their rucksacks, packed with a four-day log, felt like a ton. The RTOs were bent at the waist, temporarily easing the load on their shoulders. The birds came in, one behind the other, momentarily blowing the men on the initial lift back with a gust of wind and sand. In a few seconds they were airborne, however, headed for the planned LZ.

Once everyone was on the ground the CO gave Bill the mission to check out a URS (undefined radio signal), located about eleven hundred meters away. From the grid location he gave the LT for this site, Bill calculated his azimuth and proceeded to relate the assignment to his men before they moved out.

Although the VC and NVA had nowhere near the support and organization the American units enjoyed, they were extremely clever in their methods of operation. Since they operated in small, seemingly unorganized groups, some means of communication was essential for their coordination. In many cases the URSs served as this coordinator.

Generally very crude, the URS site was often nothing more than one or two transistor radios, with wire strung out a certain distance for the antenna. One or two individuals would manage the site for a period of time, but normally they moved around regularly. Some of the U.S. helicopters were equipped with electronic gear to pick up signals coming from these sites. While not usually pinpointing the location, they could give a general estimate of the source. This estimate was stated in terms of a radius. If the URS was said to be of an alpha radius, it meant that it was within two hundred meters of a certain grid point on the map. The radii increased as uncertainty increased, terminating with a foxtrot radius URS, which was somewhere within ten thousand meters of a certain grid location. Thus a foxtrot radius was detected but not pinpointed.

It was an extremely hot day. The ground was wet from the heavy rain of the preceding week. The Third Platoon started out at a pretty good pace, but by noon, when they set up for lunch, a number of men were suffering from heat exhaustion. The combination of the heat, heavy pack, and a week's layoff was really taking a toll. Bill rested them longer than usual, for he didn't want to risk a medevac, or contact, when they were tired. One twelve-inch-wide trail had been found up to this time and it had negative recent use.

Continuing on their original azimuth, they came across several more trails, but none of these were recently used either. Because of his limited tracking ability, Bill relied solely on his experienced point men and squad leaders for interpretation of these trails.

Unless the activity in a certain area was heavy, as it was in and around a bunker complex or village, most trails in the jungle were of the broken brush type. These were extremely difficult to read, primarily because no footprints remained. There was still information to be gained, however, for the direction of movement was determined by the way the vegetation was trampled. A rough estimate of the number of individuals passing through was calculated by observing how packed the trail was and by its width. Time of travel could be estimated by inspecting the broken vegetation. If the vegetation was dry one could surmise that the trail was not used for some time.

When hard-packed, well-used trails were found, boot or slick imprints were normally detected. This often provided the added information of who had come through the area. The NVA wore boots similar to the GIs', and these had a distinctive sole. The VC wore slicks or sandals, often made from worn-out automobile tires, and this also left a distinctive imprint on the ground.

The going became slow and exhausting. Bill's point man seemed to turn back toward him every one hundred meters, his face dripping with sweat, to ask for a break. The LT always paced himself and the platoon by the speed and fatigue of his lead man, so they stopped each time the point man needed a rest. The vegetation was so thick it was like walking down a dark alley, where sound was the only warning of something present.

It was about 4:00 p.m. Up until then they hadn't found very much of anything, when all of a sudden the point man froze in his tracks, motioning to Bill that he had spotted something. Dropping to his knees, he waved to the LT to advance and take a look.

They had gone more than a mission finding little more than a trace of the enemy. While he didn't consider himself becoming lax, subconsciously Bill held onto the hope they would continue finding little or nothing. With the point man's signal, however, his hope was shattered. His suppressed fear became a stark reality. It was a feeling akin to nothing he'd ever experienced before. This was a situation that the training fields of Georgia could not simulate. It was a situation where one's mind struggled to erase emotion, struggled to logically analyze the situation without the benefit of past experience or knowledge.

"Bill, tell tango and Charlie to drop their rucks and keep quiet. We've got movement ahead," the LT said, his heart beginning to pound against his chest. He crawled up to his point man as Bill, the LT's RTO, called back his instructions.

"What have you got?" the LT asked softly but nervously.

"I can see a poncho straight ahead LT, and one off to our left," Mazz whispered.

"I saw somebody duff out the back way," Gonzales added, crouching low on the LT's left.

Peering through the heavy brush, the LT verified the sighting of ponchos, but he was not sure if the gooks were still around.

"Stay down for a moment."

Bill turned to his forward squad leader.

"Chuck, get your squad on line. We definitely have something in front of us."

The LT crawled back to the radio. The RTO had the long whip up and said the CO had been on the horn.

"Three-three, this is five-five, over," the LT said, his voice cracking a bit.

"Three-three, tango, go."

"Roger, put the three-three on."

There was a moment's pause.

"Three-three."

"Roger, this is five-five. We've got a camp of some kind here, with ponchos up. One of my pennies saw somebody duff, so I want to crank up on the mortar, over."

"Roger, I'll put the eight-three on."

"Five-five, five-five, eight-three," the mortar section RTO said moments later.

"Roger, crank up on alpha three," Bill replied, his eyes gazing around the area. His mind was beginning to fill with fear that they had walked into something bad. Chuck's squad was on line by this time, and he wanted to recon by fire. The LT told him to wait until the fire mission was complete.

Candidates in OCS were taught three methods of reconnaissance, all of which were used in Vietnam. Map reconnaissance was nothing more than studying an area by looking at its representation on the map. Aerial and ground reconnaissance represented two others. Sometimes the latter two employed recon by fire, especially when it was believed the enemy was still present, even though they could not actually be seen. Weapons were fired at the suspected location in hopes of inflicting enemy casualties, or at a minimum, warding off a potential contact.

Everything the men were doing was Bill's responsibility, his decision. He felt very unsure of his tactics and leadership ever since the point man stopped.

Adjusting mortar fire into the rear of the suspected campsite, he saturated the area before calling an end of mission. Crawling back up to the front squad, the LT could tell Chuck was impatient about sweeping forward.

"OK, Chuck, recon by fire and move slowly ahead. Be sure to keep everyone on line."

He said nothing to the LT, but motioned his men to open up. The quiet afternoon was broken by the deafening sound of machine gun and '16 fire, ripping leaves, vines, and branches, and even splitting small trees. Slowly the men moved forward. Bill joined them, duck-walking all the way.

The fire continued until they found themselves in the middle of a small complex. Setting up all around security, they noted down everything they found. The other squad remained where they had been from the beginning, their only function being security of the rucksacks and rear.

It took about an hour to gather all the information required for a sit rep, and to destroy some of the things they found. As it turned out, this was a radio transmitting station, complete with horizontally laid antennas, transistor radios, and a living bunker containing a crude kitchen. The coals in the fire were still warm, giving the grunts assurance that someone had occupied the site shortly before they arrived. Whoever it was didn't waste any time leaving the scene.

"OK, Chuck, take the radios and let's go. We have to find an NDP and call this stuff in." The LT was noticeably less nervous and afraid at this point.

After spending a quiet and dry night some one hundred fifty meters away, they planned their day's activities over breakfast. Bill decided to take the same squad back to the URS site to complete its destruction. On their return the other squad would find an LZ. They could then backlog the radios and a few documents they thought brigade might find interesting.

The first part of the day's activity went smoothly, but with no suitable LZs in the area, they were forced to chop and clear their own from a rather small clearing. Utilizing C-4 explosive tied to the trunks of about twenty trees, they barely made room for one bird to land. This task took most of the day, and by the time the items bound for the rear were finally backlogged, it was time to find another NDP.

The gooks were clever at monitoring the activity of American units, so it was never wise to use the same NDP for two successive nights. Charlie could fix the GIs' location, pace off the distance to his tube, and mortar the hell out of the grunts when they were least expecting it.

To the southwest, in the distance, the men could hear Blue Max working out against a suspected bunker complex. It was a successful day for Bill's platoon. They had succeeded in walking right into a URS. More importantly, they were able to capture some equipment and documents. Morale was high as the NDP was prepared that night. They were anxious to get a report from Brigade S-2 on their findings.

Brigade S-2 was the intelligence section of the brigade command staff. It was responsible for the receipt, analysis, and reporting of all materials and information related to enemy activities. Information came in the form of situation reports. They included reports from the field, aerial observations, captured documents, and information provided by POWs. The materials were synthesized as quickly as possible and then provided to the appropriate personnel in the form of intelligence.

Two days later, moving heavy, the Third Platoon came upon what appeared to be a bench made from small trees. This was, in all likelihood, an observation post. The gooks employed them when they occupied bunker complexes or any temporary position. The OP (an individual) was placed on the outskirts of the complex, and he could hear or see anyone approaching. His function was to serve as an early warning against intruders. The grunts were correct in their assumption. In the same area they found two latrines, nine bunkers, and two tables, all of which looked fairly old.

It was difficult to see Charlie's bunkers, but often you could tell one might be in the area. The VC and NVA required water, just as the GIs did. But the enemy didn't have the logistical support, so they had to remain relatively close to streams and rivers. Use of a particular area for any length of time began to leave signs, that is, well-packed trails, trash, and cuttings. Cuttings were trees, approximately six inches in diameter, which were sawed and used in the construction of a bunker. Fresh cuttings, of course, indicated newly constructed or rebuilt bunkers, and usually a high probability of occupation. Old cuttings would indicate the possibility of a complex, with no assurance of any recent habitation.

A well-constructed bunker had a separate entrance and exit, with enough room inside to stand and move around comfortably. It had about three feet of overhead cover, made of logs and dirt. It was camouflaged from aerial view by pulling and tying trees directly overhead. Dug so that really only the roof was above ground, these bunkers were almost invisible. Often the point man was stepping on one before he even saw it.

Searching a complex was time consuming, with a relatively high danger factor involved. Everything found had to be called in to battalion in the form of a sit rep. The men searched bunkers one at a time, ensuring their approach was not directly in line with the entrances and exits. Fortunately, up to this time, the Third Platoon never found one occupied during a search. The possibility always existed, though, along with the demoralizing chance of hitting booby traps. Obvious pieces of equipment left behind by the enemy were prime components of such booby traps.

Once the scope of the complex was determined and preferably mapped, important documents, if any, were policed up and the report was sent in via radio. Often the platoon leader called for a kick out of demolition too and destroyed the bunkers with cratering charges. These shape charges of high explosive not only destroyed the bunker, but more importantly, blew away all the vegetation overhead, leaving the area open for aerial observation.

It had been a busy day for the platoon, but they set up that night again feeling a sense of accomplishment. The grunts completely destroyed the complex, making it impossible for the enemy to use that jungle motel for a long time.

The following day was spent moving, for the CO and the Fourth Platoon had just CA'd to a new location. Bill had orders to close in on them. It was easy moving, though, for the area was very open, with nothing to slow them down but elephant grass. In the late afternoon, the LT had them stop and set up their NDP. It bothered him somewhat that they had to set up in the open, with little cover in the event they were hit.

"We've set up in worse places than this, LT," was one reply Bill received to his question of the merits of his choice for NDP sites. He walked the perimeter and talked to his men while it was still light. None of them were really concerned about being in the open. He still felt uneasy about it.

Just before dark, while the men were putting out their trip flares, a definite humming sound was heard. The sound was getting louder and louder as it approached their position. Glancing upward, they noticed a huge swarm of bees flying overhead. The bees, thank goodness, continued flying into the sunset.

Bill had the mortar section, some fifteen hundred meters away, fire two reference points for preplanned fires before it got too dark. He found it easy adjusting the fire because he could see the rounds impacting the ground. Normally this was never the case.

The entire night remained quiet and dry. The mosquitoes, however, didn't just fly by like the bees. They were terrible as usual.

9

The land remained fairly open as the platoon continued to move heavy all through the next day. Toward evening a decent spot to spend the night was found. There was enough room within the perimeter to facilitate movement to the guard positions, but thick enough to provide concealment and cover.

It was just getting dark when Bill received a call from the Fourth Platoon. The way Bill had his location plotted, he was set up about five hundred meters northwest of them.

"Are you still moving?" LT Thorp inquired.

"That's a negative. We're in our NDP," Bill replied.

"Well, I've got beaucoup people walking in front of my position."

This was the beginning of a sleepless night for the men. Walking through an old abandoned firebase, right in front of the Fourth Platoon's position, were an estimated one hundred individuals, comprised of NVA, VC, and people in civilian clothes.

"They're moving toward the whiskey," Thorp added.

"Roger, got a solid," Bill replied, swallowing hard. His heart was beginning to sink into his stomach. Heading west, it meant they were coming right toward him. He proceeded to alert his platoon sergeant and squad leaders.

LT Thorp decided not to engage with organic weapons, but elected to bounce Blue Max instead. It seemed like an eternity passed before Max came on station. In the meantime, the enemy continued to move west, now situated somewhere between LT Thorp and Bill. It had become dark. Bill's men were lying still, praying the enemy would not walk into them. Within a few minutes the long file of the enemy could now be seen by the Third Platoon, just to the south of their position. They continued to move west but fortunately were not aware of Bill's men just a few hundred meters away. Bill estimated the number to be seventy-five to one hundred. He and his men remained perfectly still and quiet, just hoping not to be discovered. The platoon would have been overrun by that number of enemy, even with the firepower the Third Platoon had. It was a tense and scary moment, to say the least.

"Snowball seven-five, Snowball seven-five, Reddog two-niner, over."

"This is Snowball seven-five," LT Thorp replied softly.

"This is Reddog two-niner, identify your location, please," the Cobra pilot commanded.

"Wilco. Stand by for illume round."

"Roger, keep it continuous. Break, Snowball five-five, Snowball five-five, Reddog two-niner, over."

"This is five-five. I'm standing by with illumination," Bill replied.

One of Bill's men stood next to him, his M-203 grenade launcher pointed straight up in the air. He was ready to fire the first round when Bill gave the word.

"Roger, I want it continuous," the pilot reiterated.

The platoons fired illumination rounds and hand flares until they had none left.

"I need continuous illumination," the pilot commanded again to the platoon leaders. "I can't fire for you unless I confirm and maintain your locations."

"Build a fire in the middle of your perimeters," the CO told his LTs. He was working with the Second Platoon some distance away but was monitoring the radio calls.

"I don't have any C-4," Bill replied.

"I don't care what you use, just build that fire and keep it going," the CO retorted.

"Roger," the LT crisply replied.

The grass and branches of trees around them were wet from the afternoon rain and that added to their anxiety. Somehow, though, with the help of heat tabs (flammable pellets used to heat C-rations) and their flammable mosquito repellent, the Third Platoon got a small fire going. Naturally it gave their position away to everyone, but if Max was to work for them, they had no choice. The Fourth Platoon was able to build a similar fire in their perimeter.

"Reddog two-niner, Snowball one-zero, over"

"Reddog two-niner."

"This is Snowball one-zero. Have you got two fires on the ground now?" the CO inquired.

"Negative. I've got at least four fires, over."

Bill couldn't help but think the gooks were monitoring, and had built fires of their own, just to confuse the situation even more. In reality, though, the problem originated from the use of a flare bird. This helicopter had come with the gunship, and thought it was helping by dropping flares to illuminate the area. Some of the flares failed to burn out before hitting the ground and had ignited small fires when they landed.

With determined effort the men in both platoons kept their signal fires going, and when the flares on the ground finally did burn out, Max was able to report two distinct fires. This certainly now gave the grunts a little relief. Identifying the friendly locations, Max told the LTs he was about to roll in.

They all got down low as he came in on his first pass, firing ten-pound rockets into the dark jungle below. He was aiming between two orange-yellow balls of flame that marked the friendly positions. Shrapnel whizzed through the trees just over their heads. Thorp began immediately making corrections when he saw where the rounds made their impact. The pilot appreciated the quick adjustments, for it didn't take him long to get in position for another pass. Thorp could only guess where the enemy was now that they were being fired upon.

"Ensure you have my location," Bill nervously told the pilot. "We're getting lots of shrapnel and I'm afraid anything closer will hit us directly."

The LT's ear was getting tired and sore from the radio handset pressing against it. But he continued to coordinate his position with Max. His immediate goal was to ensure there would be no friendly fire this night.

"Roger, I have a firm fix on your location," the pilot replied confidently.

He rolled again, the fiery trail from his rockets very distinct against the black sky. Shrapnel came in really close again as the rockets thundered on impact. The LT's men did nothing but hug the ground. All feared not only the possibility of getting hit by Max, but movement to their front again, detected by one of his men, indicated that the enemy was quickly on the move but still near their position.

Max rolled a few more times before informing the LTs he had to break for POL (fuel). Another gunship quickly took his place, though, and fired on a few more passes before Thorp called an end of mission. Max stayed on station, however, circling high above, in the event Bill now needed him at his location. About two hours passed. The movement experienced earlier had ceased. The enemy must have totally dispersed from Max's onslaught, Bill surmised. His mouth was bone dry from the continuous radio dialogue. Jim Talbert came over to him with a canteen of water. The purified, muddy water never tasted so good.

They still anticipated that something could happen so sleep was pretty much forgotten. Too scared to risk anything but short naps, the men just continued to monitor the area. They remained flat and still. During the previous week they hadn't seen much of anything. Now, all of a sudden, it seemed the world had caved in on them.

"LT, Gonzales is outside the perimeter and has a .45 with him," one of Bill's men whispered. The LT was still sitting in the middle of the perimeter, next to one of the radios.

"What?"

"Yeah, and he must be having hallucinations because he's talking out loud to himself, saying something about the fires."

"Have Chuck get him back inside the perimeter and send him over here. Be careful."

Bill didn't know what in the world was going on with John, but hoped they could quiet him down. The rustling noise of men now walking inside the perimeter bothered the LT. He still felt the gooks could be close, close enough to hear the grunts if they weren't careful. Chuck managed to get John disarmed and brought him to the middle of the perimeter.

"Listen, John," the LT said, "sit down here and help me monitor the radio."

"I heard gooks out there, LT. They're still out there, I know they are."

"Listen, I know you're afraid. We're all afraid. But the best thing we can do right now is keep still. We have the advantage, John. We're set up and they can't see us. But we've got to remain quiet."

John finally settled down and leaned sideways against the tree where the radio lay. He and the LT remained silent for a short while. Bill hoped he had convinced John that he wasn't alone in his fear, and that he was now safe with his buddies around him.

Max left station about midnight. The platoons extinguished their fires and just sat back, listening for signs of movement. There was no need to tell anyone to maintain security, for all were too afraid to do anything but wait for the sun to rise.

Captain Silver called as they sat in silence and asked the LT for a sit rep. Bill told him things were quiet. The CO said the same was true for him and for Thorp. The radio conversation seemed to settle John down even more. He now had his eyes closed and was drifting off to sleep.

Bill sat back and thought of his first night in the bush, when he too was imagining all sorts of gooks creeping around. Tonight he could truly empathize with John.

"Chuck," Bill whispered, crawling over to his first squad leader's position. "Pair your men up on the perimeter. Don't let anybody remain alone."

"They're paired already, LT, and everybody's awake."

"Fine, and make sure Torres does the same."

"Roger."

By keeping his men paired, the LT felt it would relieve some of the tension and fear. There was some comfort in knowing you had a buddy next to you, even though he was probably just as scared as you.

Returning to the radio, Bill noticed that John was still dozing. He, too, leaned back against the tree. When his eyes opened some time later, the early morning sun was shining. They had survived the night. John was sound asleep, curled up under a poncho liner next to the LT. Bill picked up the handset of the radio and waited for the CO to call. He usually talked to his three LTs at first light. In the distance, a small loach could be heard sweeping the general area. They were probably following up on the enemy movement from the night before. A short time later the LT had his platoon sergeant check to see that everyone was awake. The men then proceeded to pack their gear and make ready to move out. There was no desire to eat breakfast. Fear never did much for their appetites.

The CO instructed Bill to link up with the Fourth Platoon. This was welcome news for Bill. He felt it was safer having two platoons moving together, especially when the enemy was sighted in such unusually large numbers. It turned out, however, that the main reason the CO wanted them to link was they were tentatively scheduled to CA to another location. It was much easier for Yellow One to transport the larger group.

The Third Platoon moved almost due west for five hundred meters, based on the heading Max had given them from the fires. Bill recalled that he had plotted himself northwest of the Fourth Platoon. This, he thought, was the main reason for his anxiety and fear of Thorp's gunship adjustments. He couldn't picture clearly in his mind how the corrections were affecting the rounds in relation to his own location.

It didn't take long to reach the Fourth Platoon perimeter. The LTs sat down to briefly discuss that eventful night. While awaiting word on the CA, Thorp pointed to where the enemy broke into the open. He said about fifty passed in front of him initially, across the flat, open area of the old firebase. After a short break, another group of approximately fifty individuals followed. Bill couldn't blame him one bit for staying down, not desiring to engage them. There was a good chance he could have been overrun, even with the element of surprise in his favor. Had I been in his position, Bill thought, I would have done the same thing.

Rain began falling as late afternoon approached. Not sure whether Yellow One would be in to get them if it kept raining, they decided to set up their hootches. The Fourth Platoon took half of the perimeter, Bill's the other. No sooner did they have their hootches up when the hard shower tapered off. The CO called moments later to tell them to make ready for the CA. Repacking their wet gear, they moved out onto the old firebase to await the arrival of the birds.

Bill laid down on his back, thinking about the previous night and how lucky they were. He couldn't remember being so scared in his life. Another quick shower ended a brief appearance of the sun. The raindrops fell gently on the LT's face and clothes. He pulled his boony cap over his eyes, content to let the rain soak his fatigues. It was getting hot now, and the rain provided some relief. The men were getting ready to start an operation in a completely new area, but this wasn't going to immediately alter the memory of that nerve-racking night just passed.

10

Two days after the move Bill found himself supporting the Second Platoon. They were on a mission to destroy a known bunker complex. The platoons moved out light, early in the morning, from the company-size patrol base. Walking in a long Ranger file, Bill's platoon moved behind the Second.

The complex was calculated to be about eight hundred meters away, but they found a large network of logging roads early in their search. Following one of these roads, they swept the area without finding a single bunker.

There were many woodmen, or loggers, in Vietnam, whose livelihood was cutting timber. They transported the timber by truck to mills, where it was made into lumber. The trucks were driven right into the dense jungle from the villages. After a period of time, their trucks created crude roads. These roads wandered all over the place, but they were generally of no use to the grunts. It was tempting to walk on them, however, since they provided easy movement. But they were considered dangerous because the men were exposed more so than when they were breaking brush.

Turning off the road onto a much less traveled one, the platoons halted when the point element of the Second Platoon reported seeing what appeared to be a gook on OP. He was sitting right on the edge of the same road on which they were walking. From monitoring the radio, Bill learned that the individual ducked onto a trail that branched off the road. The point element went out on a light escapade, hoping to track him down. The remainder of the men had stopped and were awaiting further instructions.

The day was beautiful. The bright sun began to heat up the jungle, quickly drying the wet leaves and grass. On the ground, the ants were already busy with daily chores, while termites concentrated on old, fallen trees that abounded in the area.

It wasn't long before Bill was instructed to move his platoon up the hard-packed trail. Although the point element had lost sight of the gook, they did locate several bunkers at the junction of two trails. Following the road, and then the newly discovered trail, movement was easy, especially without the added weight and bulkiness of a rucksack. The Third Platoon moved partway down the trail before linking up with the rear element of the Second Platoon.

Walking in the middle of this large group of individuals, the LT could empathize with his men, for they always said they never really knew what was going on. This was true, for if you were not up front to see what was happening, little information was relayed back to those in the middle and rear of the formation.

A few moments later Hoss called Bill up to the front, to brief him on the situation. Bending over at the waist to avoid the limbs and vines that hung over the trail, the LT quickly made his way to the front of the file. Hoss, his RTO and several others were crouched down in a large ravine, located to the left of the trail. The ravine terminated at the base of a large tree. It provided some shade and cover for a huge bunker only a few meters away. Maintaining a low profile, Bill slid down into the ravine and approached the LT.

"My point squad is out in front, Bill," Hoss said softly, pointing in the direction they had gone. "They located a few bunkers and want to recon by fire."

"OK," Bill replied.

"Get your people down and give me an up when you're ready."

"Roger that."

Crawling back to the large tree, Bill told his point and slack men what was going to happen, and to stay low. They passed his instructions back down the trail on which the remainder of the platoon was positioned. Hoss had his men in front of the first bunker and along the ravine to his left. Once certain all were given the word, Bill crawled back down into the ravine, signaling the LT his men were ready.

The word was given to the recon squad and they began firing. To the horror of everyone, the fire came right in on the platoons, shearing branches and leaves with the blast of a machine gun and several M-16s. At first Bill thought the gooks had outwitted them and were now firing on the grunts, but that was definitely not the case. Instead, the recon squad had become disoriented, and was now firing at their own men. Bill quickly turned to Hoss with a puzzled look on his face. But Hoss was immediately aware of the dreadful mistake.

"Cease fire! Cease fire!" he yelled.

The firing stopped seconds later and immediately the call for a medic was heard. One member of the Second Platoon was hit in the thigh by a '16 round. Quickly moving to the tree where his people lay, Bill anxiously asked if anyone had been hit. The point man said no, but complained of a burning on his leg. The medic checked him out and found he too had been hit, but fortunately it was only a graze. Luck was surely with him, for the tree just above his head was riddled with bullet holes. The top of a plastic mosquito repellant bottle he had stashed in his shirt pocket was shot clean off.

The smell of expended ammunition filled the air all around. Everyone was upset about the whole thing. They just wanted to return to the CP. While it was fortunate no one else had been hit, it was impossible to even justify why two men were wounded. What if those men had been killed? Bill thought. Why did we even bother to get up this morning?

A medevac was called to evacuate the two men. While waiting for its arrival, the bunker complex was mapped. The number and size of each bunker was carefully recorded. A large pot of rice, still warm, was discovered, indicating they had interrupted the daily activity of several individuals.

It didn't take long for the medevac bird to arrive. Once the men were lifted out, the platoons organized themselves and prepared for the return to the CP. The LTs now had the difficult task of explaining to a very irritated CO exactly what happened.

Later that day the battalion commander came out to the patrol base. After his departure, Bill learned from Hoss himself that he had been relieved of command of the Second Platoon. This was very upsetting to Bill because he didn't feel it was Hoss's fault. What happened out there could have occurred to anyone. However, since an LT is responsible for his platoon, he has to bear the burden and consequences of that responsibility.

There was nothing Bill could say or do to ease the agony Hoss felt inside. He was a devoted platoon leader, a conscientious and warm person. Bill told him he would speak to the CO on his behalf and did so later. However, Captain Silver said it was the battalion commander who had made the final decision.

It was truly a discouraging day, one that really exemplified the tragedy of war. How do you explain to the parents their son was wounded in an all-American firefight? Could they believe, and even accept, that a dreadful mistake like that happens in combat? These were the thoughts that entered Bill's mind that evening. He had no answers, and neither did anyone else. It seems the men had run out of luck. Things had been going almost too well for them. Maybe something like this is bound to occur, Bill thought, and today was our day.

Reconnaissance of the area continued over the next two days, searching for suspected bunker positions. Each time Bill went out he preplanned mortar fire, calculated the distance they would travel, and determined the appropriate azimuth. He learned an important lesson from the incident two days prior. Be certain where your men are at all times, especially when you have several elements moving in close proximity. Use marking rounds or jungle como if you have to, but know where they are located.

The Second Platoon already had a new LT. Dick Beahm, a West Pointer and new in country, was anxious to take over and carry on the missions. He too came to the bush with no experience, and would rely heavily on his men for the first few weeks.

The company was extracted the following day. But as Bill's platoon was to learn, it would have been better staying in the bush. Mace was the main firebase and a relatively comfortable one at that. Unfortunately, it couldn't accommodate all the platoons. Two platoons had to occupy and defend a mini-base south of Mace called Hall. The Second and Third platoons now had the pleasure of living there for a period of four days.

Hall would not have been bad during the dry season. But it was the monsoon season and the men were greeted by mud six inches deep as they departed the birds that brought them in. The mud immediately began to cling to their boots, making them feel like blocks of lead. Those who didn't slip and fall, especially at night when you couldn't see a damn thing, had exceptional balance and luck. The sleeping quarters left a lot to be desired too. Metal culvert, topped with several layers of sandbags, was called home. Ammunition boxes served as a floor so the men didn't have to sleep right in the mud and water.

Hall had a bourn just like all the other bases, but the wood line was only one hundred meters away, much like old Charles. The firebase was extremely crowded because of its small size. It did have a lot of firepower, however. One battery each of 105s and 155s, along with a mortar section, provided the grunts in the bush with good support.

Trying to sleep on this base was quite an experience. The grunts had pretty much gotten used to the wet weather and the pounding of artillery at night. But the noise and feel of rats running around and on top of you was something else.

Scraps of food that accumulated in the hootches attracted those unwanted creatures, and it was a never-ending battle to get rid of them.

During the day the sun seemed to start drying things out, but the afternoon and evening rain, almost as faithful as Old Faithful, managed to make things miserable again. It seemed there was no way that Hall was ever going to dry out. It was often funny to see the men slipping and sliding as they got in line for chow. More than once someone would take a header while carrying food back to his hootch, having to get back in line and try all over again.

Guard watch, especially on this firebase, seemed to generate as much fear and uneasiness as it did in the bush. Despite the fact that there were a few lights on within the perimeter throughout the night, along with the constant hum of a generator, it was pitch dark all around the outskirts of the base. This made it easy for a guard's mind to wander, to believe someone was creeping up on his position. An illumination round was fired periodically from the mortar tube and lit up the area fairly well for a minute or two. This seemed to reassure the guards, if only briefly, that no one was out there. The flare would slowly float to the ground on its small parachute. Guards would peer left and right, trying to spot that possible sapper who was coming up on their position. The verse from their training days was again weighing heavily on their minds.

> Vietnam, Vietnam, late at night
> while you're sleeping, Charlie
> Cong comes creepin' around,
> Vietnam.

The flare settled to the ground, creating unusual shadows amid the trees and vines along the wood line. When it finally burned out, all became black again, rekindling the uneasiness in their minds.

Rain normally fell lightly throughout the night. Water always seemed to drip from the roofs of the bunkers onto the guards' backs, soaking through their clothes. Soon they would start to shiver. It was easy, under these conditions, for them to feel lonely and sorry. They would think about their friends back in the world, sleeping in a warm, comfortable bed, without a care. Something didn't seem fair about that.

Ironic as it sounded, the men in the Second and Third platoons looked forward to the day when they would CA back into the bush. The men occupying Mace understood that desire, for Hall would be their home the next time around.

11

Fortunately the days at Hall passed quickly and soon the company found itself about to CA on another mission. Following a trouble-free insertion, the men set up in a company-size NDP, amid human skulls that marked the scene of a previous battle long since over. There were many trails in the area, but most were fairly old. The night was not a quiet one, for while Alpha camped in relative solitude, a village to their west was hit by VC. The grunts could hear the thundering of Max's rockets and blurp of his mini-gun. The United States was once again spending thousands of dollars to quell the intense desire the VC held for victory.

Bill's mission, as the sun rose the next morning, was to cloverleaf southwest toward the Song Luc River, and then toward the LZ they used the day before. The Second Platoon had not CA'd with the company, but instead had to pull extended security on another firebase. They were coming in later that day, though, and it was Bill's job to secure the LZ for them.

Movement was slow, for the vegetation near most rivers was always thicker than elsewhere, making headway deliberate and exhausting. Bill stopped about five hundred fifty meters out of the CP and set up a hasty patrol base. The FO was with him and he called in a 105 mission on the LZ while the men were set up in the base. It was more or less a formality to prep an LZ before a unit was inserted. It was never known what might be waiting in ambush.

The Second Platoon was due in about one o'clock. It was already noon. Bill still had to move seven hundred meters along the river to reach the LZ. He called the CO and instructed him to delay the insertion about one and a half hours. This, he hoped, would give his platoon enough time to reach the LZ and secure it.

They picked up and moved immediately after the fire mission was completed, receiving confirmation of the new insertion time as they traveled. The river was more winding than appeared on the LT's map, and this made their trek still more difficult. About 1:30 p.m. helicopters were heard in the vicinity of the LZ. Vegetation was still too thick to see the birds. Bill just surmised someone back at battalion failed to get word on delaying the insertion. Sure enough, when he called the CO, Captain Silver said Yellow One had the Second Platoon aboard and was waiting for the Third Platoon to arrive. There was no way Bill could reach the LZ at that time, and the CO realized this. Consequently, Yellow One was instructed to fly back to Mace and wait for the LT's word. What a waste of blade time, Bill thought, as they trudged along.

Arriving at the LZ about 2:00 p.m., tired and frustrated, the men vowed never to move along a river again. That, of course, was just wishful thinking. About a half hour later the Second Platoon landed. Bill led them to the CP, following the back trail the company had made the day before. The ground was wet and soggy most of the way, compounding the misery of an already sorry day. Not long after reaching the CP, the company moved about three hundred meters to an NDP site. Rain started falling as they set up their hootches. It was another night in which the men would sleep in wet clothes.

It rained just about all night but remained quiet. The sun tried to burn through the thin cloud cover early the next morning. Alpha was making ready to recon southeast, this time along the Soui Luc River. Oh no, here we go again, Bill thought. The mission was changed before anyone had moved out, however. Instead, the company was placed on alert for Operation Rome Eagle. This meant they had to be within thirty minutes' traveling time of a three-ship LZ. Rome Eagle was an operation employed to counter threats to the major population centers. Since the overall mission of the First Cavalry Division was to defend the Saigon, Long Binh, and Bien Hoa areas anyway, Rome Eagle meant danger was imminent. United States and Vietnamese officials feared there would be trouble during the country's elections. They wanted infantry units available on short notice should the cities come under attack.

The Second Platoon and mortar section were instructed to move south to find and secure such an LZ. The rest of the company remained in the NDP site. After noon chow Bill decided to clean his weapon, damp from the night's rain. No sooner had he cleaned and reassembled it when AK fire ripped through the perimeter. The men all hit the ground in a sudden moment of surprise and fear.

"Where do you want the gun?" one of Bill's men yelled, running across the perimeter with a machine gun, despite the continued fire.

"Over here," came the reply.

The LT got up and quickly ran toward the sound of the voice. His mind was telling him they were pinned down. The men were lying as flat as they could, shooting off rounds at nothing but the thick brush. It was impossible to really see anything. Diving behind a tree, close to the initial contact area, Bill hugged the ground, straining his neck to attempt to see an undeniably coy and cunning enemy.

"Anybody hit?" he yelled, gazing left and right. There was no reply.

"Get some ammo up here, goddamn it!" someone angrily shouted.

In a moment, several men with belts of M-60 ammo crawled to the gun that had done all the firing. Random bursts of M-16 fire rang out to ward off any attempt of force by the invisible gooks. The CO, in the meantime, had bounced Max, Rash, and a Pink Team. Continuous smoke poured out of the perimeter, as each came on station and unloaded his costly array of ordnance into the surrounding jungle below.

After the air power show Bill took a squad out to sweep the area. The CO accompanied him, supervising a search that reminded Bill of his training days, when shouts of "On Line, OK, Move Out," filled the training fields of make-believe soldiers and bunkers. With no success, they returned to the disorganized and disrupted perimeter, now filled with the smell of smoke and expended ammunition. It wasn't until they returned from the sweep that Bill learned one man in the Fourth Platoon had been shot in the wrist. He was in good shape, though, but also very lucky the gooks weren't more accurate in their aim. The bullet had gone through a log before it hit his wrist.

The men were angry at themselves and had every reason to feel that way. Here they had one man hurt, expended thousands of dollars in ordnance, with nothing to show for it but their carelessness. The gooks must have been monitoring them for some time that morning, finding it easy to creep up close to Alpha's position. The grunts didn't employ any OPs to provide early warning against such an event. Furthermore, and most importantly, they were too lax and noisy. The lesson had to be learned the hard way.

Operation Rome Eagle was cancelled later that day. Unconcerned about finding an LZ, the company moved south about four hundred fifty meters. They linked up with the Second Platoon and mortar section and set up for the night.

The next morning Bill's medic had the most trying experience of his short time in the bush of Vietnam. He had gone outside the perimeter to relieve himself when he observed a gook tiptoeing slowly across an overgrown logging road. He was moving away from the company position. The gook hadn't seen Doc, but there was no doubt in Doc's mind what he now had to face. Raising the ever present M-16 to his shoulder, he had the dark, mean-looking gook in his sights but couldn't pull the trigger. He feared getting friendly fire from within the perimeter. He had told a few of the men he was going out, but more than likely they hadn't told everyone else. To compound the problem, he was standing only a few meters from a claymore mine. If blown at the sound of fire, it would have scattered him all over the jungle.

In the span of probably ten seconds the gook, dressed in dark green and black, disappeared into the dense jungle, still unaware of his foe behind a rifle a short distance away. In an instant Doc was back inside the perimeter. Breathless, he related his experience to Bill. The LT got a quick patrol together and combed the surrounding bush. Doc was able to point out where the gook had stood. They found slick tracks on a small trail which led toward the perimeter. A poisonous bamboo viper appeared on the trial as well. This snake was light green in color and about two feet long. Bill decided to conclude the search and head back to the perimeter.

The medic was noticeably shaken up by the whole matter, blaming himself for not having blown the gook away. Bill reassured him, though, that it didn't matter since his life was also in jeopardy. It wasn't worth the chance.

There was normally a fine line between accomplishment of the mission and welfare of the men. LTs had been taught to put mission before welfare. Because Bill was not convinced the U.S. presence in Vietnam was actually accomplishing anything, he couldn't always accept the code. He had to act to protect his men if he felt the danger was just too great.

Over the next few days the men were resupplied and continued to patrol the area. The patrolling produced very little in the way of evidence of recent enemy activity, even though they knew from experience the gooks were in the AO. On one such patrol, however, the Third Platoon came across an old General Motors truck, bearing the almost completely weathered insignia of some American religious organization. How it got there was, and would probably remain, a total mystery. There were no navigable roads to be seen. The jungle, of course, grew continually, so a road could have become overgrown in a relatively short time. Not too far from the truck they found an oxcart, reminiscent of the old American West. They were very common in the villages of Vietnam. Bill had an amusing time calling in a description of the truck, saying the rusty, dilapidated thing appeared to have negative recent use.

Bill's patrol was cut short when his point man, Joe Mazzatenta, walked right into a wasp nest. It was built shoulder high in the thick brush. The men scattered momentarily, as wasps flew all around, anxious to take revenge on their intruders. Stung in the neck and head, Mazz began shaking all over, a reaction he had never experienced before. Calling the medic up to the front, the LT became worried watching Mazz tremble before his eyes. Doc rubbed him down with antiseptic powder and instructed the LT to head back immediately. They did just that, getting back to the perimeter as quickly as possible.

Along with wasps and snakes, the grunts also had to contend with ants and scorpions. If disturbed, they could really make their presence known. The LT recalled sitting down at a guard position one night, unaware that he was sitting right in the middle of a nest of black ants. Within seconds he was bitten all over his body. He literally had ants in his pants. Some of the men would take their boots off at night and put on boony slippers. One of Bill's squad leaders was stung by a scorpion that had crawled inside a boot. The sting was extremely painful, almost paralyzing for a period of time. Sometimes on patrol the grunts would also come across huge spider webs. They could be six feet in diameter. Right in the middle of the web sat the spider, about five inches long, generally black and yellow in color. It would have been quite a shock for the point man to walk into something like that.

Rain began falling late in the afternoon as the LT read some letters from home. It was another wet night to sleep in the bush. The following morning the company CA'd into a different area, based on new intelligence. URSs indicated elements of the Thirty-third NVA. The LZ was green but the men had to put up with the usual hassles of platoon sectors of responsibility. It remained cloudy all day but rained very little.

The denseness of the jungle made many things difficult, including the construction of a patrol base or NDP. It was bad enough constructing a perimeter with one platoon, not to mention the problems associated with a company-size base. Arguments, confusion, and lack of security were the trademarks of the effort to set up in one large perimeter. The CO would tell the platoon leaders their sectors of responsibility. However, while in the process of positioning the men, the sectors would shift, either pushing out or closing in, depending on the thickness of the vegetation. Needless to say, each platoon would blame the other for not conforming to the original plan. For a while nothing would get accomplished. Finally, after a compromise or two, the platoons would somehow link together, forming the oddest looking triangular or circular perimeter anyone could imagine.

Bill moved out with his platoon a day later to recon northeast along a river that flowed adjacent to Alpha's perimeter. It was raining as they left on their all-day escapade. All along the way the LT's glasses continually fogged up. The platoon was fighting its way through a rain-soaked jungle almost beyond description. Bill's glasses were really of no use to him so he angrily jammed them in his shirt pocket. It was one of those mornings when he woke up in a bad mood and stayed that way most of the day. They covered nine hundred meters and didn't find a damn thing. Before he returned, the LT decided to give the mortar section a little workout. He called for a fire mission on one of his preplanned targets. He let his RTO call them in and do the adjusting. Bill felt a situation could arise where he was unable to make the call and someone would have to do it quickly. Since the RTO was always at the radio it was good experience for him. The men headed back to the CP once Bill was satisfied his RTO knew what to do.

"Thanks for letting us fire for you, LT," came the voice of one member of the mortar crew as the Third Platoon walked back inside the company perimeter late in the afternoon.

"Hey, you guys did a fine job, putting them right where we wanted them. And my RTO was doing the adjusting," the LT replied. He was in a better mood by then. The mortar section certainly appreciated it when they could work for their fellow grunts. At no time did Bill ever lose confidence in their ability or the support they could give him.

12

The first of October had arrived. The Third Platoon remained in the perimeter that day while the others patrolled. The morning sky was filled with clouds and the wind blew very hard. In the distance the men could hear rain falling, moving in their direction. Hootches were tightly fastened in preparation. Bill felt sorry for the men on patrol, for there was no way they were going to remain dry.

The days passed by slowly when the grunts were just sitting in one place, but it afforded Bill the opportunity to discuss a number of policies with his men. He always enjoyed talking with them, getting to know a little about their backgrounds, opinions on the war, and future goals. About sixty-five percent of them were volunteers and the remainder draftees. Their average age was about twenty-two. Some had wives and children waiting for their return home. None really knew why or whom they were fighting, but they had a mission, nonetheless, and they were determined to carry it out. It was a shame they had to spend their enlightened years, as Bill called those same years of his life, in a foreign land. But the fact of the matter was they were in Vietnam and nothing was going to change that. Their only reimbursement, other than the meager pay received each month, was the time they could call their own. They read books, wrote letters, and often just spoke their minds about a myriad of subjects to their buddies. The comfort of a hot meal and mail came every four days. Naturally it was looked upon with eagerness and enthusiasm. There was no denying the fact these men were homesick from the day they left American soil.

The grunts wore the same clothes for a week or more, and slept on the ground amid leeches, ants, scorpions, rats, spiders, and snakes. Life in the bush was difficult, so little things like a cup of coffee or hot chocolate helped to ease the thoughts of being dirty, cold, and miserable. Because they had to remain alert to any and all signs of the VC and NVA, they were never able to fully relax and enjoy the tranquility and sheer beauty of the jungle that surrounded them. Despite the physical elements and the anxiety associated with having to live minute by minute, never knowing what was going to happen next, the men were dedicated, energetic, and seemingly fearless in their approach to everything.

"How's it going, John?" Bill asked as he knelt down next to one of his men. He was laying against his ruck, reading a Western novel.

"OK, LT," he replied, gazing up at the LT's face, almost without expression.

"Guess the other platoons haven't found anything," Bill said as he looked out into the thick brush and trees that helped conceal their position.

"How long we gonna be here, LT?"

"Couple more days, I imagine. Most likely till we've covered the area to the CO's satisfaction."

"Any word on drops?"

"Not a thing, but hopefully when we get back to the firebase they'll have some word for us about early outs."

"Sure hope so. I wanna go home." His eyes were now back to his book.

"So do I. So do I," Bill replied, getting to his feet and moving toward two other men along the company perimeter. "Gol'darn, everyone's reading today."

"Not much else to do, LT," one said, smiling.

"Did you clean your weapons?"

"Roger that," they both replied, almost in unison.

"You guys are new in country. I wondered how you were adjusting to this place."

"Well, I wish we wouldn't hump so far each day," one replied.

"Yeah, and that ruck is much too heavy," the other added.

"I know what you mean. My platoon sergeant almost drove me into the ground my first week in the bush. That's why I always tell you guys to stop me when you need a rest. I'm not out to break any speed or distance records. I just want to get the job done, but ensure that you make it home safely too."

"How long we gonna be out here, LT?"

"We'll be going back to Mace in about eight days."

"Oh, we're not going to Hall?" one asked.

"We'd better not, it's not our turn!"

"Well, I guess we can survive then," the other replied, a smile forming on his sunburned face.

"Hey, by the way, where are you guys from?"

"I'm from New York."

"Florida," said the other.

"Get any mail yet?"

"No, not yet, LT. How long does it take?"

"Well, it took me seventeen days from the time I mailed my first letter home, but you'll get one soon."

"Sure hope so," one replied softly, his eyes peering off into the jungle.

Breaking through some thorns and bamboo, Bill reached one of his gun positions where his assistant gunner sat making a midday meal.

"Jack's out taking a leak, LT, so don't fire him up," Howie said, grinning as the LT approached. Bill could hear the bushes moving out to the front.

"O.K. Hey, what are you making?"

"Beef and rice, LT, it's my favorite."

"Yeah, it's my favorite too."

The LT sat down next to a book and some newspapers piled near their hootches, only two meters from their gun. Howie poured a half cup of hot water into a plastic bag of dehydrated rice and beef chunks. Bill watched his dexterous hands peel off pieces of an onion and a pepper he managed to acquire on the previous log day. Mixing the whole thing together, he carefully folded up the bag and placed it inside the outer bag to simmer for a while. He looked around, momentarily puzzled, and then picked up several packets under his leg and proceeded to pour cocoa and sugar into the other half of his canteen cup of hot water. Just then Jack, the gunner, appeared, a .45 caliber pistol holstered around one side of his waist and a Bowie knife on the other side. He used the knife to clear brush when they put up their hootches.

"How ya doing, Jack?"

He sat down without replying right away, grabbing the papers he had left at his hootch.

"Can't complain," he finally said, dryly.

A few drops of rain began to fall on the leaves over their heads.

"Oh shit. Has to rain just when I was going to eat."

"Yeah that's always the way," Bill replied with a laugh as he got to his feet.

"Hey, LT, let's go back to the firebase today."

"OK, Jack, I'll call the birds right now," the LT replied, smiling. Turning, he almost ran into one of his squad leaders who was carrying a radio.

"What's the problem, Torres?"

"Nothing, LT, I'm just gonna use our radio on OP."

"Roger that."

Bill walked to a position normally occupied by the Second Platoon, but now, in their absence, being covered by one of his men. It continued to rain lightly but most of the drops were absorbed by the vegetation overhead. John Gonzales sat propped up against a small tree, reading a rather thick paperback. He was so absorbed he hardly realized the LT had approached him.

"What are you reading?"

"Oh, a mystery. Not too bad either."

The LT again gazed out at a wall of trees and brush.

"How much time have you got left, John?"

"Forty-seven days and a wake up," he quickly replied, proud to admit his shortness.

"You sure must have seen and been through a lot during your tour."

"You know, LT, when I die I'm sure going to heaven cause I've already been to hell."

"Boy, I guess you're right," Bill replied, thinking to himself how true that statement really was for many of them.

"You must be able to see a big change in the war now, compared to the way it was when you first arrived."

"I sure can, LT. The new guys must think the war's over. They're noisy, don't care about security and don't know what to look for on patrol. I'm really afraid to go out with them. Is there any way I can get a job in the rear, especially since I'm so short?"

"I don't know, John, but I'll check for you. Listen, I'm counting on you guys with all the experience to talk to the new people. Tell them what they're doing wrong. Show them what to do."

"I just want to get the hell out of here," he replied somewhat angrily, turning once again to his mystery book.

Bill was still too new in country to really know how John felt deep inside. He walked over to his medic's hootch where Doc was seated and writing letters.

"Hey, Doc, have you or Jim heard from Washington yet?"

"Not yet, LT, but we should be getting a response soon. The senator from my home state is against the war, so I know he will support me."

"That's great."

Doc and several other men had been writing their members of Congress, calling for an end to the war. Their letters also served to clarify exactly what the grunts were doing in Vietnam. Most people back in the world believed the GIs were just sitting on firebases, waiting for the freedom birds.

It was necessary, from the grunts' point of view, to make the American people aware that they were still actively patrolling the jungles of South Vietnam.

Theoretically, of course, the men were defending the firebases, but defense of a firebase required active, offensive patrolling. The base would otherwise have been vulnerable to VC and NVA mortars and rockets, some of which had ranges of more than five miles.

Some of the men had received encouraging responses. A few members of Congress said they would make an effort to clarify the GIs' position to the American people. Several of the hawks, however, replied with strong disagreements to the stand Bill's men took regarding American involvement. This only served to increase the number of letters written by the grunts, though, so was not taken as a setback of any kind.

The men truly hoped the American people would not become apathetic, and let Washington continue on its course. The sooner the people realized their involvement in Vietnam was a hopeless situation, the sooner they would effectively pressure Washington to get the men and women home.

One might ask why the grunts like Doc, Jim, and others did their job, despite such feelings of animosity toward the war and American involvement. The answer is simple. Refusal to go to the field meant LBJ (Long Binh Jail), and the excellent possibility of a bad conduct discharge from the Army. While an honorable discharge never really benefited a GI later in civilian life, a dishonorable discharge was very influential. The grunts were puppets on the field of battle, with Uncle Sam holding all the strings.

Finishing his rounds, Bill stopped at the CP to monitor the radios. The CO was out with the Fourth Platoon and had left him in charge of the perimeter.

"Neither platoon has found anything, LT," Mac said as the LT approached.

The LT sat down on an ammo box, leaning up against a tree near the CO's hammock. He kept his M-16 in his lap.

"Yeah, I guess it's been pretty quiet in the AO all day."

Picking up an old edition of the *Stars and Stripes*, Bill read the headlines, which reflected some of their combat operations. The paper also contained news from home. The men always hoped of one day reading that the war was over, that peace had finally been negotiated, and they could go home. He looked up and realized the light rain had stopped almost as quickly and unnoticeably as it began.

"Mac, you've been over here for a long time, haven't you?"

"Yeah LT. It'll be eleven months soon."

"I was speaking to Gonzales about the war, back when you guys first came over. He said it's changed a lot, particularly noticeable in the attitude and actions of the new men."

"I would agree. We don't see as much contact now, so it's hard for the newbies to stay focused and constantly on guard."

"Do you like working in the CP?"

"At first I did, but now I'm bored and want to hump a gun again."

Mac was a machine gunner before becoming an RTO, but even after acquiring the radio he kept his gun. Talk about a gung ho grunt!

"LT, I'm gonna speak to the CO about getting out of the CP. Could I join your platoon if he'll let me leave?"

"Sure."

"You know, I was in LT Matulich's platoon before you came. That's when we had the First Platoon too."

"Yeah, how come they did away with it?"

"We got in a contact in July and lost quite a few men. They just divided up the guys left and assigned them to the other platoons. We've never gotten enough replacements to form the platoon again."

"Huh, I never knew that."

"So I'm going to talk with the CO and see what he says. I hate just sitting around here monitoring the radio all day. Besides, I've got to get a step-on before that freedom bird takes me home."

"Hey, I have to laugh every morning, Mac, when I hear you on the horn saying pop smoke, that's my bird."

"It's funny, LT, but just about every morning at first light a freedom bird flies into Bien Hoa. We must be getting a lot of replacements now."

The commercial jets that brought personnel to and from Vietnam made a loud, whining sound as they approached Bien Hoa Air Base. Often the grunts could see them too and in their minds wished they could be flying home on one. To the grunts they were not jets but freedom birds.

Mac soon received word that both platoons were on their way back, having had no luck finding Charlie. Bill got up and alerted his people on the perimeter, telling them to expect the platoons at any time. He relayed the direction they gave for their return. About twenty minutes later the men heard the crashing of brush, signaling the approach of at least one of the platoons. By five o'clock both were safely inside the perimeter.

The day had been uneventful for Alpha Company, but to the south a sister company had walked into a bunker complex and suffered one man killed. Cobra gunships had been called to the contact area as the sun slowly began to disappear. A radio on their push provided some interesting listening. A few of the men sat near the mortar pit, watching the gunships work.

The CO called the commander of Charlie Company and informed him Alpha's mortar was prepared to help them if they needed support. This made evident the rapport that not only existed at the company level, but also within the battalion. Every grunt in Vietnam was there for a cause. If help was needed by anyone there wasn't a moment's hesitation. The men slept that night with artillery fire continually pounding the contact site. It was something they had grown accustomed to over the past weeks and months.

One afternoon, a few days later, Bill was on patrol, searching an area just north of Charlie Company's contact site. He began to see indications of a bunker complex. Hard-packed trails, fresh cuttings and a river nearby told him to proceed cautiously. A little farther along there appeared to be fields of fire cut, indicating the presence of fighting positions. The gooks cut fields of fire leading out from their bunkers so they would have unobstructed, yet camouflaged lanes down which to fire their weapons. They succeeded in doing this by cutting away the vegetation growing knee high or less, leaving the taller trees and shrubs in place to camouflage their bunkers and the surrounding area. A point man normally would never suspect fields of fire until it was too late. The only way they could be detected was to get down in a prone position and visually check for them. The lanes would lead directly to openings in the bunkers.

Alpha's sister company had walked into a complex two days ago and Bill wasn't about to do the same thing. He backed off about one hundred meters, setting up a hasty perimeter. Calling on his mortar section back in the CP, they cranked up on one of his preplanned targets. After adjusting a few HE rounds in on the suspected bunkers, the LT called for a fire for effect. The mortar crew responded by dropping five consecutive rounds right on the suspected target. Monitoring the area for a short time afterward, the men could see no evidence of movement. The lateness of the day cut short Bill's desire to move ahead and visually check out the results of the indirect fire. They had to return to the CP before darkness completely set in.

While they hadn't confirmed the location or existence of a bunker complex that day, Bill slept better that night knowing he hadn't openly risked the lives of his men by walking into a potential trap.

13

Before long the mission was over and the men were back on firebase Mace. It was always a welcome change from the bush. The men could get cleaned up a whole lot better, they slept better and, of course, they got three hot meals a day. But Bill also took the opportunity to hold a platoon formation, at which time he broke the unit down into three new squads. He scheduled rifle range training for all his men too. Intelligence reports predicted the battalion would continue to operate in the same AO through February. Activity in the area was not expected to change very much.

One evening, during their stay on Mace, Bill had an interesting human relations discussion with the CO. It all began when Captain Silver learned that the LT had sent four of his men to the rear a few days earlier than usual for DEROS. Bill had to justify his reason for doing this because there was a great amount of pressure on unit commanders to keep their field strength up. While a certain percentage of the grunts were always in the rear due to hospitalization, leaves, R&Rs, and DEROS, a close eye on this percentage was maintained at battalion. If it became excessive the unit commander quickly heard about it and had to provide an explanation.

In defense, Bill pointed out that they had done a fine job for him in the field. Since they were not going to CA with the company again, there was no reason for holding them on the firebase. In the rear they could relax without the artillery blasting their eardrums. They could also prepare for their flight home. After all, they had given twelve months of their lives here, spent almost entirely in the bush. How could a few extra days for themselves have harmed anyone?

The CO, of course, didn't see it that way. Had every platoon leader decided to do what Bill had done, the battalion rear would soon have become overcrowded. Furthermore, there was always plenty of work to be done on the firebase, so every available body was needed.

It was battalion policy that seven days prior to DEROS an individual reported to the rear for out-processing. In most instances, though, this provided the minimum time needed to make all the arrangements, particularly when transportation was not available to the individual. The facilities he had to clear were scattered all over the post.

The LT could clearly understand the CO's point of view, but at the same time he wanted to take every opportunity to make things as easy as possible for his men, given the sacrifices they had just made. While the four he had sent to the rear would not be requested to return to the firebase, Captain Silver made it very clear that, henceforth, Bill act in accordance with the rules laid down by battalion, regardless of the circumstances.

They continued to talk about policy matters, broadening their discussion to include the notion of how well a platoon leader knows himself, his men, and his responsibility toward the overall mission of the battalion. They agreed that there are many factors, not all clearly defined and understood, that influence the thoughts, actions, and emotions of an individual in a combat zone. Certainly a person's upbringing and experiences help shape his character and contribute to his overall behavior and value system. In order to fully understand someone, then, requires an understanding of his value system. Obviously, we can't even fully understand our own value systems, let alone those of others. Thus we oftentimes question our own actions or inactions, as well as those of others. Rules and regulations can help shape and contain our behavior, but sometimes they run counter to our value systems, and then problems develop.

The CO and LT concluded that, at best, some understanding of an individual can be attained through observation, communication, and recollection of past performance, but that was only scratching the surface. From their own observations and recollections of past missions, they were able to categorize the men in a superficial sense. They concluded the men could be placed in one of three groups, each having certain characteristics of performance.

The "Gung Ho" individual was one who looked forward to each mission and the opportunity to kill gooks. He was not necessarily a volunteer to Vietnam, but the majority in this category did enlist for combat duty in Southeast Asia. While they didn't like to be hassled or assigned to work details on the firebase, commanders never had to worry about their refusing to go to the bush. These men found the battalion rear to be boring, a place where time seemed to stand still. The gung ho type often asked to walk point, probably the most dangerous and physically demanding job they could have chosen. Some of the men who fit this description grew up on the streets of major cities.

The "Typical Grunt" was one who always did his job, whether it was carrying an M-60 machine gun in the bush or filling sand bags on the firebase. While he never liked being hassled by anyone, he never disobeyed an order, unless, of course, it was personally degrading. Some were against the war and naturally did not wish to fight. They were essentially marionettes in Uncle Sam's combat theatre. While most in this category would have jumped at the chance to get back to the relative safety of the battalion rear, none went out of his way to do so.

The "Shammer" looked for every opportunity to stay out of the bush. He used all conceivable means to attain his desires, including telling lies to his superiors. He was satisfied to remain on the firebase if he could get away with it. But his main goal was to get to Bien Hoa and somehow remain there indefinitely. If he could arrange to miss the log bird or a CA, he would be able to spend three or four fewer days in the bush. Barring a few exceptions, everyone was really a shammer at heart, but the men labeled as such had to be closely supervised on a continual basis.

One of the primary means to a successful sham was to cleverly fake an injury difficult to diagnose. For then it was the patient's word against the doctor's. Typical injuries included bad backs, knees, and feet. Some of these men would not take their malaria pills, hoping to contract the disease. It meant a thirty-day sham, at the very least. Others would not take proper care of their feet, hoping to get trench foot or some other infection. The medics on the firebase and in the rear seemed to be very willing to grant profiles and future appointments to all who visited them. This, of course, didn't help matters for the commanders. It seemed they were continually at battle with the medical profession.

Bill recalled an incident while on patrol, when one of his men just stopped and refused to go any farther. They were moving heavy and the guy kept complaining of his knees. He was jeopardizing the safety of the LT's men and the success of the mission. Bill had to finally just tell him they were going to leave him behind. Not wishing to remain in the jungle all alone, he agreed to press on and the platoon completed its mission. When they got back to the firebase Bill sent him to the rear for examination. The LT never saw him again. It didn't bother Bill, though, for the guy had been a continual hindrance to the rest of his men. Was he a shammer? Bill would never really know for sure.

The discussion went off on a slight tangent as the LT and CO talked about the best way to handle human traffic to and from the rear. Normally the stay on a firebase was four days. This was generally not enough time to adequately handle the myriad of problems that arise in a company of eighty to a hundred men. What they were trying to do was work out in their minds a fair and viable policy. After tossing around many ideas, they concluded that three possible solutions existed, each having its own strengths and weaknesses.

The first system allowed only one individual at a time to go to the rear. This minimized the number of personnel in the rear, which was the main goal, but it meant that those with urgent needs would have to wait their turns. A partial solution to this problem was to bring the people who could solve their problems to the firebase. This meant arranging for people trained in finance, medicine, and other fields to be on hand when the company arrived on the firebase. The main weakness of this policy was that there were times when these traveling consultants didn't make it to the firebase, even when all the arrangements had been made. The grunts could then do nothing but bear their problems a little longer.

A second policy the LT and CO pondered would send any number of men in. It was obvious that a control factor was required in the rear to make this system work. It meant that some of the permanent rear personnel would have to act more or less as chaperones, to ensure that once an individual's problem was solved he proceeded back out to the firebase and not to some hideaway in the rear. This was particularly necessary if a shammer was sent in. The obvious fault with this policy was the potentially large number of people it allowed in the rear at one time. This placed an extra burden on the clerks, who were already swamped with work. It also had the potential to drop the lance of commanders to a dangerous level.

A third solution was to leave it up to the platoon leader's discretion whether he thought it was necessary for the individual to go to the rear. The weakness here was the platoon leader's judgment. If he mistakenly sent in a shammer, other men with legitimate problems would suffer. If he refused to let someone go in, thinking it was a sham, but it really wasn't, it could exacerbate the problem.

The first policy, even with its inherent weaknesses, seemed to be the most fair and viable. How it would work in practice only time would tell. Certainly some system had to be developed, for mental, spiritual, and physical problems always existed. Whether they were real or contrived, each had to be considered and evaluated in the fairest and most realistic manner possible.

Their discussion concluded on the point about understanding one's responsibility toward the overall mission of the battalion. The CO felt Bill didn't fully understand his responsibility and what the battalion was trying to accomplish when he sent the four men in early. In the LT's opinion, though, how well a platoon leader understood his responsibility toward the mission of the battalion was contingent on the leader's belief in the mission itself. While most everyone understood the overall mission and responsibility, not all honestly could say they thought it was correct. Bill, for one, had many doubts about his role, and that of his men, as defender of freedom and democracy in a foreign country. Should the United States have been so deeply involved in the affairs of the Vietnamese? Could it be that we wanted democracy for them more than they wanted it for themselves? Because these doubts existed, Bill always put the welfare of his men first. Only if the success of a particular mission was obviously crucial would he sacrifice their safety.

The rap session ended when the CO was requested to report to the TOC. It couldn't have come at a better time, for it would have been futile to debate the issue of mission over welfare when there is no right or wrong in a debate about beliefs.

14

The men had an enjoyable but busy three days at Mace. Tomorrow they would CA once again. The insertion point would be based on a URS, known bunkers, sensor readouts and a sighting by the Pink Team. It seemed almost inevitable they were going to encounter some action.

The mail clerk managed to make it out to the firebase during their stay but the finance team didn't. Bill learned that the men would now be paid either midmonth or just before Vung Tau. He reported this to his men as part of the operations order given late in the day. Sergeant Holtz described the new three-squad concept of movement and NDP setup.

A light drizzle fell from an overcast sky the next morning as the grunts waited on the pad for Yellow One to arrive. The weather provided a perfect description of their enthusiasm and interest in this new mission. Around 8:15, despite the cloud cover, they lifted off and moments later were on the ground, amid fresh trails running in all directions. Moving as a company to the southwest, they walked right into a recently abandoned bunker complex. After carefully checking the entire area, they set up a perimeter. There appeared to have been five living bunkers in all, and probably occupied until the first few artillery rounds fell during the prep. The complex was only a short distance from the LZ. The rounds had most likely frightened all the occupants. Freshly cooked rice and other foods were found. The grunts knew the gooks didn't leave food behind unless they had to leave in a hurry.

Having established the perimeter, each platoon was given the mission to search in a particular direction. Bill moved out to the east. It wasn't long before he began finding numerous hard-packed trails, most of which ran north to south. This was contrary to what Alpha expected, because the villages were out to the west. Continuing on, the LT moved his platoon a little more toward the north and came upon a hootch or shelter of some kind. It was difficult to say whether this old, lean-to type hootch, with its hand-tied branches, was used as an OP or provided shelter for a guide. The VC used guides to lead men and supplies through an area unfamiliar to all but the guide. Moving a little farther along, they soon found themselves on the outer edge of an old bunker complex. In all, they were able to locate and map nine bunkers, each one completely filled with water from the monsoon rains. Footprints, however, and empty cans of food, indicated that the VC and NVA were using the area anyway, and not too long ago. They probably slept in hammocks outside the bunkers. The Third Platoon returned to the CP in the late afternoon with quite a bit of information to relate to the CO.

It rained heavily that night, but by morning the sun was shining. Bill's mission that day was to recon northwest. Before they moved out, however, the CO gave the LTs a briefing on rules of engagement. Since they were operating near South Vietnamese villages, they had to be sure civilians were not fired upon. Anyone carrying a weapon was considered enemy, but all others created the difficult job of ascertaining identity. They were to base this identity on the dress of the individuals, as well as papers they carried. Bill thought about the LT Calley case throughout the entire briefing, as did the other LTs. In March 1968 LT William Calley entered the village of My Lai with his platoon and proceeded to massacre twenty-two innocent villagers. In a 1970 court martial he was found guilty of premeditated murder and was initially sentenced to twenty years in prison.

Bill decided to move out early, for they had a long patrol ahead of them and he didn't want to get back too late. LT Beahm and the Second Platoon trailed Bill part of the way before breaking off to cover their designated area. The terrain was flat and very much open. Elephant grass, brownish in color and four feet high, swayed gently in the breeze, much like the Midwest wheat fields of home. Scraggly looking trees dotted the area also, providing contrast and a sense of depth to the openness. Visibility was about two hundred meters, a rare but welcomed occurrence. This didn't lower security, however, for unseen ambushes could have been set up in the high grass, to await the arrival of a patrol such as theirs. The sun overhead was hot as they moved in a Ranger file, tramping down the grass into a distinct trail, the type of trail they were looking for. The men couldn't help but make good time in the process.

"LT, someone in the rear said he had movement on our left," said Bill's RTO, walking right behind him. They had traveled about seven hundred meters. The LT glanced in that direction but failed to see anything except grass and a tree line bordering the open area far to the northeast.

"I don't see anything," he replied, turning his head back toward the RTO as they kept moving. Continuing to look that way periodically, all of a sudden the LT saw four heads bobbing up and down, just barely visible over the grass. They were moving perpendicular but toward the platoon.

"Torres! Torres!" Bill yelled, trying to get the attention of his point man who was totally unaware of the movement. Torres continued on the azimuth, crashing down brush twenty meters out in front of everyone. He was unable to hear the LT's trembling voice. The slack man heard him, though, and turned back toward Bill. But he too was unaware of the sudden, desperate situation. Glancing to the left again, Bill's mind filled with concern. Whoever they were, if they continued in the same direction, would run head-on into the point man. Would Torres remember the rules of engagement if they were civilians? Bill anxiously thought. Fear and worry about Torres climaxed in the instant they saw each other.

"Dong Lai!" Torres shouted, telling them in Vietnamese to stop. But in the same moment he raised his M-16 and unloaded his banana clip in their direction. The sharp, cracking sound echoed across the still, flat land. Running up to him, the LT reached a logging road where he found his squad leader bending over a woman. Blood covered her left arm, which was almost completely blown away. The other three individuals were running back in the same direction from which they had come.

"Get the medic up here! Mike, call the mortar section and tell them to stand by."

"Roger, LT."

Bill was hoping to trap the fugitives in a barrage of indirect fire, forgetting his M-203 men would have been quicker and more effective in halting their escape. The medic and another squad leader worked on the woman as the LT got on the horn to adjust some rounds into the wood line, the apparent objective of the three fugitives.

"Sarge, get the men in a perimeter around the woman," Bill commanded, his eyes combing the immediate area. He was trying to think of too many things at once. In a few moments a perimeter was established and the first few mortar rounds were falling. Bold adjustments had to be made to bring them somewhere near the spot they thought the three may have entered the wood line.

"Torres, the CO wants to know who they were," Bill said, as he turned to see his squad leader bending over the medic. Torres was noticeably concerned about the woman's condition. He came over to the radio and took the handset from the LT.

"Three-seven, this is five-five tango, over."

"This is three-seven, how about a sit rep."

"This is five-five tango, uh, I was walking point when I saw four gooks coming down a logging road toward me. One was a woman, two looked to be NVA, and the other was an old man, over."

"Roger, did they have weapons?"

"That's affirmative. The two NVA carried carbines but I don't remember if the old man had one. The woman jumped in front of them when they raised their weapons. I aimed for them but she got in the way, over."

"Roger, good work. Put the lima tango on again, over."

"LT, we need an urgent medevac," Doc said, as Bill took the horn from his squad leader.

"Roger, OK, listen up. Spread out a little. Everybody's too close. If they try to sneak up on us again we'll be in trouble."

"Three-seven, this is five-five," Bill said, still looking around and concerned about the possible chance they, or others, might try to creep up through the grass and hit his platoon.

"This is three-seven, how ya doing, buddy?"

"This is five-five, roger, uh, we need an urgent medevac, rigid litter, for the female. Tell the mike section they did a fine job, over."

"Roger, I'll get the medevac out to you right away."

LT Beahm called seconds later and said he had come upon a very fresh trail. There were bare footprints of one to three individuals heading northeast. The discovery of several pairs of slicks near the woman just about confirmed the footprints to be those of the fugitives.

After medevacing the female, along with a cloth briefcase of clothes, food, and documents, the Third Platoon continued on in a Ranger file to the northwest. This was the direction in which they were traveling when they were so rudely interrupted. Normally the LT would have changed course and tracked the gooks who duffed, but the Second Platoon was already doing that so Bill just stayed on his original azimuth.

The platoon was forced to stop after traveling about four hundred meters farther. The brush had become too thick to make any headway. Rash happened to be circling above, so Bill picked him up on their push. The LT told him he was bogged down in heavy vegetation and asked if he could show them an easy way out. The LT popped smoke and in a short while was given a heading that took them out of all that shit. Bill thanked him for his help and the platoon quickly picked up a hard-packed trail that brought them back to within one hundred meters of the CP. It had been a tiring day for all of them, but the men were pleased to have captured a POW. They hoped she was going to provide brigade with some valuable information.

It wasn't until eleven o'clock the next morning that Alpha was back to normal operations. Up to that time the company had to remain in defensive posture because of the lack of air assets. A historic prisoner exchange with North Vietnam that morning required most of the aircraft. There was to be no patrolling for Bill's platoon anyway. It was again his turn to secure the company perimeter while the other platoons ran escapades. The colonel came out about four o'clock and had a partial readout on the female POW. The men learned she was 99 percent VC and a commo liaison between the VC and NVA elements in the area. Information she carried and divulged was more political than tactical in nature, but she did provide brigade with some interesting notes and letters. Torres was very happy to hear the news. It meant the woman had survived despite her wounds. Also, she was able to provide some information that brigade could use. The LT hadn't talked much with Torres since the date of her capture but Bill noticed his squad leader had been bothered by the whole incident. Torres was in a life-or-death situation that day yet it bothered him to know he had actually shot someone. Bill didn't seem to understand why Torres felt this way, but then the LT had never experienced a situation like that. How would he have reacted?

The following day was a busy one for the Third Platoon. Bill remained with the CP as the other platoons moved to a new LZ. Just after midday the grunts destroyed four of the eight bunkers that surrounded them. The cratering charges threw logs, branches, and leaves high into the bright blue sky as they exploded. The men tightened up the perimeter with the absence of the other platoons. They worked hard, despite thick brush and a pouring rain, to clear fields of fire, paths to the guard positions, and lastly, spots for their own hootches.

Bill's platoon was really beginning to perform like a machine these days. He was getting few replacements and everyone else had at least one mission under his belt. Little supervision was required on the LT's part to ensure that the priority of work was carried out and security measures were maintained. His squad leaders were primarily responsible for the performance of the men in their squads. In the LT's mind, they deserved high praise for a continually fine job. Day after day, they sacrificed personal time to ensure that their men were kept informed of current events and were tactically ready for any type of mission or situation that could develop.

Hoping to deceive the enemy, the Third Platoon remained behind the following day as the CP and mortar section CA'd to the LZ the other platoons located and secured the day before. Bill's mission was to destroy the remaining bunkers, including the ones he found to the east. He moved his platoon into position and set off cratering charges on four of the bunkers. Debris flew everywhere. Unfortunately, a piece of wood hit one of the LT's squad leaders. Chuck Holtz was so busy ensuring his men were behind cover that he had left himself exposed. Bill had to medevac him, for his hip was badly injured. The platoon was finally able to move out about 1:45 in the afternoon. The complex to the east was reconned again, this time with several engineers who had come along. The demolition never came out on the log bird, however, so Bill was forced to set up his NDP in the complex and resume the demolition work the next day. Tactically speaking, there was nothing wrong with setting up a perimeter (patrol base or NDP) in a bunker complex, provided the scope of the complex was known and searched in its entirety. An advantage to setting up in these complexes was the available cover each bunker provided. These particular bunkers, however, were filled with water. On the negative side, there were generally many trails running into and out of such a complex. This sometimes made it difficult to ensure every single approach was adequately covered. Alpha never made it common practice to set up in bunker complexes. But when the situation arose where the men were pressed for time, or could find nothing better, they went right ahead and set up their perimeter.

It was quiet and almost completely dry that night. The mission remained the same the next day. The platoon was to monitor the area in the morning and blow the bunkers in the afternoon. A mechanical problem with the log bird delayed receipt of the demo, however. Bill took advantage of the wait by instructing his new RTO in the call for fire. It was about two o'clock when he received instructions to abort the mission. He had to move ASAP to the CP. No reason was given for the change in plans.

It took very little time for the men to get their gear packed. Before long they were breaking brush, pushing six hundred meters very hard before Bill stopped to give everyone a break. The men remained in a long Ranger file. After resting a short time, they drove on another four hundred meters and took another breather. They didn't reach the LZ until 5:30. The LT had supper with the CO that night, discussing activities that were to begin the following morning. The CO said the mission to destroy the bunkers was cancelled because of prolonged mechanical problems with the log bird. Bill regretted not having destroyed them. In the dry season they would surely be used again by the enemy.

Darkness came quickly and everyone settled down for the night. Sometime during that night Bill's hammock gave out and fell to the ground. He was so tired from the long march that afternoon, he decided to just lay on the ground until his turn for guard came up.

The CP and other platoons moved out in the morning, leaving Bill behind once again. It was log day and the plan was for Bill to log first, giving the rest of the company enough time to reach another log site. After the resupply, he was supposed to move south, setting up a patrol base and acting as a western block. Unfortunately, the log was extremely disorganized and the platoon had to remain at the LZ until the next morning. They would then get the remainder of supplies they had requested. On a positive note, though, they did receive a visit from the pay officer, finance team, and a Catholic chaplain.

The sun peeped through the trees at dawn. Bill was still on guard duty. He observed termites moving down a tree out in front of him. In single file, they crawled along a fallen tree to his right. Apparently they were all off to work in the woods too.

The log bird came out at 9:30 with water, hot chow, and batteries for the radios. By 12:30 the grunts had backlogged everything required and were prepared to move south toward a URS. The platoon covered a total of five hundred fifty meters before setting up. Along the way they sighted two dud artillery rounds and a broken brush trail with very recent use. Once Bill got the perimeter set up he called in the sit rep of their findings. Late that afternoon the men heard movement to the northeast, which sent everyone scrambling for their positions. The movement, they later believed, was just some monkeys or baboons playing in the trees near their NDP. Morale seemed to be good. Bill could see no indication the men were becoming lax.

It could be said that every sound of movement the men heard registered "gook" in their minds. Their lives were at stake so they had to react that way. No animal impersonated a gook better than the monkeys and baboons. They often played tag with one another, running through the brush, climbing trees and swinging from vines. There were several occasions on patrol, when the men instinctively hit the ground and lay stone silent, thinking a VC patrol was approaching. All of a sudden they would hear the loud chatter of the playful monkeys.

"LT, wake up. It's time for guard."

A light rain had been falling since early evening but now was just a heavy mist. The faint light was already seeping through the trees. The air was cool and the ground wet from the night's rain. Bill hated to get out of his warm hammock, but it was his turn for guard.

"Oh, OK, Wayne, Thanks."

"Hey, LT. Rick heard the sound of a baby crying while on guard. This was about four o'clock. I called the CO and he said he wanted you to call in a few mortar rounds."

"A baby crying?"

"Yeah, that's what he said it sounded like."

"Probably two cats fighting. Uh, what direction?"

"Rick calculated about sixty-five degrees off the guard position and out about two hundred meters."

"OK, I'll call Charlie Oscar and see what he wants to do. Did you hear it in the last hour?"

"No, nothing."

"OK."

Bill picked up his weapon and carefully walked over to the guard position. His fatigue shirt was wet but his monsoon sweater underneath was still dry.

"Three-seven tango, five-five, over."

"Three-seven tango."

"Roger, five-five, is the Charlie Oscar around?"

"Wait one."

The jungle was very still at this hour. All the LT could hear was an isolated snore from one of his men on the perimeter.

"Five-five, three-seven, how do you read me, over?"

"I got you, lima chuck, how me?"

"Same, same, over."

"Roger, understand one of my pennies heard a baby's cry this morning. You want me to drop some HE on it, over?"

"Roger, drop a few rounds and check it out later."

"Roger."

"Stand by, I'll get the mike section on the horn."

"Three-seven, eight-seven, I'm on the other Romeo. I've been monitoring your conversation, over," said the mortar section squad leader.

"Roger, talk to the five-five then."

"Roger, break, five-five, eight-seven."

"Five-five, go."

"Eight-seven, we're ready any time you are. Your alpha two is about the nearest point to the crying sound, over."

"Roger, OK, give me a Wilson Pickett on alpha two."

"Stand by."

Bill gazed out into the thick brush. The early morning light was creating unusual shadows all around him. He had been sitting on his steel pot all this time and his rear end was beginning to hurt. Not only that, but his left leg had fallen asleep. He finally decided to just sit on the wet ground.

"Five-five, eight-seven, you've got a shot."

"Roger, shot."

The faint sound of the tube could be heard and he quickly shot an azimuth to it. He now knew he had to travel on a 285 degree azimuth later in the day to reach the CP. It sounded like they were about a klick and a half away.

"Five-five, eight-seven, you've got a splash."

"Roger, splash."

A few seconds later the round landed. Bill proceeded to adjust a few HE on the suspected target. The final round must have strayed because he could hear it whizzing through the air. It impacted only about seventy-five meters from his perimeter, making a loud noise and scaring the hell out of everyone.

"Eight-seven, eight-seven, five-five, over."

"Eight-seven."

"Roger, that one came in too close, buddy. Let's call an end of mission, over."

"Say again, you're coming in broken, over."

"I say again, you came in too close on that last round. I'll take an end of mission, over."

"Understand end of mission."

"Roger. Thanks."

"Eight-seven, out."

To Bill's knowledge, this was the first time the mortar crew had a stray round. Boy, it scared the hell out of him. He thought for sure it was going to land on top of them. The Third Platoon ran escapades throughout the day but nothing of interest was found. They closed with the CP about four o'clock and set up with them for the night. The NDP site was adjacent to a two-ship LZ. Judging by the foxholes dug along the perimeter and the trash scattered around, it had been used by another GI unit some time ago. To the amazement of the men, as they reflected on the day's activities, it hadn't rained at all since the previous night. Could the dry season be approaching?

15

It was October 18 and extraction was scheduled in four days. Until then Alpha planned to take a different approach to reconnaissance. Instead of the active patrolling they had been doing, they decided to try ambush positions, monitoring fresh trails and logging roads. Tactically, of course, it didn't make very much difference whether they stayed in one place and let the enemy come to them, or run patrols. The grunts had the advantage in ambush posture, though, because they would be ready and Charlie was always more prone to walk roads and trails rather than break brush. As long as they didn't compromise their position by making unnecessary noise, they had the decided edge.

Each morning the platoons were to move out from the company-sized patrol base and find a likely trail used by the enemy. They would set up manned ambushes along these trails, utilizing their organic weapons and claymore mines in the kill zone. The Third Platoon moved one hundred meters to the north the first morning and quickly found a broken brush trail running NW-SE. It appeared to have been used in the last twenty-four hours by three to five individuals moving southeast. The LT set up his ambush on this promising trail.

It was quite an experience just sitting in one place all day, waiting for something to happen. Time passed very slowly. Some of the men became irritable. Granted it was mentally tiring to remain in one spot all day, but the majority favored this to humping fifteen hundred meters with a rucksack. Bill called in a sit rep every two hours, but each time there was nothing to report. The mosquitoes seemed to be very bad here, probably more so because the men weren't moving. The weather was ideal, though, with a clear blue sky and warm sun, reminiscent of the summer days Bill spent growing up in New England. They sat back with weapons handy, eyes and ears perked to pick up any sight or sound humanly detectable. With little or no activity in the AO, however, more realistically these were days to do nothing but listen to the birds, soak up the warm sun seeping through the countless shades of green and brown, watch the normally unseen battles among the ants and other insects, and doze, with the thought of stepping onto a freedom bird back to the world. It was almost as if someone had called time out in the war. Bill transported himself back home, to his backyard, where he was enjoying the surrounding natural setting without the worry of an enemy soldier intruding. There was a chance to think about many things other than the war. Thoughts of the past, present, and future popped in and out of his mind, just as a land crab, which he was observing in front of him, moved in and out of his home in the ground.

Around two o'clock a gentle but noticeable breeze came out of the south and blew over the platoon. It cooled the men whose faces were beaded with sweat. But as quick as it came it was gone. Everything went still again. What would cause a breeze like that? Bill pondered. They returned to the CP about five o'clock with nothing to report but the bothersome mosquitoes and that unusual breeze that broke the silence and tranquility of the jungle.

It was dry overnight but the mosquitoes continued to be bad. Doc said he heard a digging sound to the north while he was on guard duty. When mortar rounds were called in he said he then heard the sound of something or someone running. Later the digging began again. Bill surmised it was an animal grubbing for food, but they would take no chances. The Third Platoon went out on patrol early in the morning to cover the area where the sound was last heard. The LT was also going to set up another ambush position.

They traveled about two hundred fifty meters north and set up an ambush on a trail that had recent use. There was some movement heard further to the north but nothing came of it. Bill had taken his bug spray along this time and it seemed to be pretty effective. He called in negative sit reps at eleven o'clock and twelve o'clock. The CO called a little while later and wanted the Third Platoon back to the CP by 3:00 p.m. The company needed to get a resupply of water from the blue to the southwest. Bill got his platoon back at three o'clock but, instead of going to the blue, they received water blivots from the log bird and extracted thirty-five quarts. In the late afternoon the LT dug a fighting position near his hootch. He felt he needed the exercise since they had been just sitting on their behinds for the last few days. He also put together a list of problems the men needed to have addressed when they got back to the firebase. After supper the CO and LT were talking about the next day's activities when a trip flare went off. It was quickly determined, however, that two big birds were the aggressors.

It was quiet and dry in the NDP and the sun shone brightly the next morning. Bill was to go out on ambush once again but return early since they were going to all get extracted the next day. The Second Platoon was coming in later in the day to join them. Before the LT moved out he coordinated several preplanned targets with the mortar section. While they were in ambush he wanted to train his RTOs in a call for fire. The platoon moved out shortly thereafter, covering about two hundred fifty meters toward the northeast. They set up an ambush position at the intersection of a trail and a stream. By noon, however, there was nothing to report. Bill had his RTOs call in the fire mission and then they packed up and returned to the CP.

At times during the mission the men heard the firing of automatic weapons off in the distance. Someone must be in contact with the enemy, Bill would often think. By the end of their third day, however, all the men of Alpha would have been upset had Charlie come bebopping down the trail. He would have interrupted their peaceful and unique look at the true beauty and serenity of Southeast Asia, a picture seen and enjoyed by few Westerners.

How foolish man is, Bill thought, the way he fights and kills his fellow man, destroying nature in the process. What makes a man want to pick up a weapon when he knows from the past it has never solved a thing? How can he keep from his mind the sorrow and pain he causes? Conflict will always exist in the world, he concluded, as long as there are two people on this earth. We're too selfish and ignorant to want to share the richness, beauty, and wonderful experience of life with everyone.

The three-day ambush, in reality, was a failure. The Third Platoon returned to the CP that last afternoon with nothing to report. It was now time to prepare for extraction. Morale was noticeably high because Vung Tau was just two days away.

Extraction day arrived and the ETA was set for 0900. It looked like it was going to be a bright, sunny day. Yellow One was thirty minutes late but soon had the company back in Bien Hoa. The LT took advantage of some free time by catching up on mail he had received. He also had to sort out personnel changes in his platoon. Sergeant Holtz and Staff Sergeant Ramsey were both still on profile and out on Mace. Hasson Kateeb and John Stone had been sent back to the United States. Bill Marks had come down with malaria. Two new people had been assigned to Bill's platoon, including his new platoon sergeant, Roger LeBanc.

Early in the afternoon the platoon test fired their weapons. After cleaning them, the men got cleaned up themselves and had a satisfying hot supper. The Third Platoon was scheduled to pull guard duty on the greenline that night but they lucked out when the order was rescinded. However, their hopes to see a movie were dashed when the projector broke down. It was a very restful night for the men, though, because they were not in the bush. Many, including Bill, just slept under the stars.

"Vung Tau, here we come!" That was the rallying cry heard the next morning as the company prepared to fly by fixed wing to the beach resort. They arrived at 10:45 a.m. where it was partly cloudy and warm. Most of the men had chow at the R&R center and then got their passes to be able to go downtown. After lunch Bill decided to hit the beach and did some bodysurfing in the big waves. After taking a shower he went to the PX with some of his men. He got a pleasant surprise when they got him a room at the Palace Hotel for $10. The platoon had dinner together at the hotel later that evening. Bill then went to see the girl he had met the last time they were here.

The LT woke up the next morning to a beautiful, sunny day. He had breakfast at the R&R center and later tried his luck on a surfboard. He found it to be much harder than it looked on TV. A party was held at the Mai Linh Restaurant that evening for Captain Silver. The CO had less than two weeks left in the bush, so this was the perfect time, when everyone was together, to wish him well. The LT then went back to the Palace Hotel where he and his men continued to party until 2:00 a.m.

Needless to say, the LT had an upset stomach and sore muscles the next day. The consumption of a lot of junk food and the surfing had done him in. This was the worst he had felt since arriving in country. The wind was blowing outside as he now lay on his cot back at the R&R center. Sand was blowing everywhere too. It was definitely not a good day to swim or lay on the beach. It was just as well, for Bill was in no shape to do either. He took several aspirin and lay back down on the cot again. By six o'clock in the evening he felt much better and attended a barbeque in the mess hall. However, by morning he was sick to his stomach again. He decided to go to the dispensary where they found he had a temperature below normal and seemed to have flu-like symptoms.

Bill left Vung Tau later that morning and arrived at Mace about one o'clock. His platoon had already left for Hall, and Bill was scheduled to join them the next day. The Second Platoon had gone back to Bien Hoa and would move to firebase Katty the next day. The CP, Fourth Platoon, and mortar were also at Mace.

The LT woke up on Mace to cloudy and warm weather. He was in no hurry to get to Hall, knowing it was probably still a mud hole. Upon arrival, however, he was pleased to see that things looked pretty good. His men were busy working on various details. Despite a hard rain later in the day, it wasn't too muddy on the base. Boy, I can't wait for the dry season, Bill thought, as he lay down to sleep that night. I don't care how hot it gets.

16

"Make sure you have the right shack sheets," Bill said to his RTO as the men made ready for still another mission. "Are you on the lift push, Mike?"

"Roger that, LT."

Vung Tau had come and gone. The sights, sounds and thoughts of combat once again filled their minds. Rain fell continuously as the Third Platoon moved eight hundred meters to the southeast from their insertion point. Bill momentarily thought of that dry, warm bed at the Palace Hotel as he walked along behind the slack man. They had to constantly brush aside the rain-soaked vines that seemed to be everywhere. It wasn't too late in the afternoon when they found a decent NDP site. The rain had stopped by this time and held off through the night. Skies appeared overcast the next morning as light slowly pierced the jungle canopy.

"Say again, you're coming in broken and distorted, over."
The LT was still on the guard position, talking with the CO about the day's activities. Commo, as usual, was bad during the daylight hours of the monsoon season.

"OK, I think I got a solid copy. Understand you want me to move sierra echo toward a bravo Charlie, over."

"Roger, you got a most solid copy. Move whenever you're ready, over."

"I got negative further."

"Negative further, out."

The men were very slow in their preparation, trying to let their wet clothes dry out a little. No significant trails were found as the platoon moved to higher ground. Bill set up a patrol base and took out an escapade to the south. He didn't find anything and returned to the NDP site early. Commo became better as evening approached. His lance was twenty-seven men, the highest it had been since taking over the platoon way back on the fourteenth of August.

A call from higher (battalion) the next morning instructed the company to be in PZ (pick up zone) posture ASAP. The men were used to such changes in mission, so it was no big thing. They never knew the real reason for them, however, this go-round being no exception.

It was 9:30 when the platoons reached an open area large enough for an extraction. They were very close, as a matter of fact, to the area where Bill's platoon had captured the POW. After a VR (visual recon in a helicopter) and a briefing with the colonel, the CO informed his men they would not CA. Instead, they would NDP near the PZ and extract the next day. They were going to be inserted somewhere else. The grunts slept to the beat of a light rain falling on their ponchos and artillery pounding an area about three klicks away.

After what seemed to be twenty changes in mission that next morning, Alpha was finally prepared to CA. The reason for the changes was because a sister company was in contact, having walked into an occupied bunker complex. This was Charlie Company again, as luck would have it.

"Two low birds shot down with three killed and four wounded," Bill told his men as he moved from one group to another on the PZ. He had been monitoring the radio during Charlie Company's contact and tried to relate as much of it as he could before his people lifted off. All were now ready to be picked up. Bill's platoon was going in first.

"Remember, we're covering the north side of the LZ," he said, briefing his last group.

At two o'clock they hit a green LZ but automatic weapons fire could be heard from the contact area in the distance. An air strike was called in while the men got organized on the ground. They finally began moving and covered a total of five hundred meters before setting up in company size for the night. Artillery pounded the contact site seventeen hundred meters away. The gooks must have something in there they want, or they're just plain stupid, Bill thought, monitoring a radio transmission the following day. A low bird still spotted individuals in the bunker complex despite the air strike and artillery.

After a second air strike, which included napalm, the men moved toward the complex, setting up their NDP in platoon size. All three platoons were fairly close to each other. LT Thorp had left the bush on the log bird earlier in the day to become the company XO in Bien Hoa. It was well deserved and surely welcomed by Wes Thorp. LT Bill Mitchell was now in charge of the Fourth Platoon.

Bill set his Third Platoon in near a river, amid some fresh, hard-packed trails. He was operating with three squads, so his NDP took the shape of a triangle. An M-60 was placed on each of the corners and served as the primary guard positions. These positions were in strategic locations. One afforded a clear view of the river without being exposed. The two others covered trails that ran to the river from different directions. Claymores, of course, were out all around. The men were entirely locked in with each other. For once they had good commo with the other platoons. LT Mitchell, being the rookie, was with the CP.

Bill had opened up a beef hash LRRP and was heating the water near his hootch when all of a sudden one of the machine guns began firing. With the LRRP flying one way and his hot water the other, the LT dove for the ground, grabbing his M-16 instinctively.

"Anybody hit?" he yelled over the noise of the gun and '16 fire. He was always conscious of the possibility of having men wounded, and wanted the call for a medevac done immediately if needed. It could have meant the difference between life and death. Crawling up to the guard position from which the firing originated, he repeated himself but still got no reply. The LT's gunner, AG, and several others were lying flat on the ground, eyes trained down a trail that lead into the perimeter.

"What's the story, Dave?" Bill asked angrily but softly, upset because he didn't know what the hell was going on. His RTO was right behind him and said the CO was anxious for a sit rep.

"We opened up on a gook bebopping down the trail, LT," Dave Moore replied.

"Did you hit him? What did he look like?"

"No, he ducked behind that tree, goddam it. Looked like an NVA with a pack." Dave pointed to a tree just off the trail, about fifteen meters away, now riddled with bullet holes.

"See anybody else?"

"No, but listen! Hear those voices?"

Sure enough, off in the distance the men could hear the sound of people talking and they weren't speaking English.

"Dave, Bobby, you, me, and my RTO are gonna go down that trail and see if we can find them."

While they quickly prepared themselves Bill grabbed the horn and briefly told the CO what had happened.

"What were they wearing?"

"Hey, Dave, what was that guy wearing?" the LT whispered.

Dave was putting a bandolier of ammo around his neck. Dennis Debickero, his AG, already looked like Pancho Villa.

"Green uniform, NVA type, but no hat."

"This is five-five, roger, we saw only one. He was wearing a green uniform but no hat, over."

"Roger, what's your plan, over?"

"This is five-five, roger, we're gonna check out the area before it gets dark. We got voices out there so they're still around."

"OK, keep me informed."

"Roger, out."

Handing the horn to his RTO, Bill rose to a crouch position and instructed his men to move out slowly. The remainder of the platoon had been briefed on his plan and quietly stood their positions. The LT really didn't want to go out there but it was the only way to positively check the area.

Moving slowly, like hunters stalking their prey, they proceeded down the trail, eyes sharp to pick up any movement, ears perked to hear a pin drop. They followed tracks believed to be those of the gook, but in a short while the patrol lost them in the dry, heavy brush. Circling around, the men could no longer hear the voices so they headed back to the perimeter. They concluded the gooks decided to move away while they had the chance. Dave definitely made him think twice about coming down that trail again, that's for sure. The gook probably told his friends the same thing.

The VC, and even the NVA, normally operated in small groups. Three, four, maybe five individuals at most, they were no match for the firepower an American platoon could produce.

Bill had no one hurt but all were jumpy to say the least. He doubled the guard that night and no one had any complaints. If there had been any guys becoming lax they weren't anymore. It appeared this mission was going to be action packed, something the men had hoped would not happen.

For the next two days rain seemed to continually fall but this didn't hinder the patrolling. Bill was now personally taking out few escapades. For the most part he was letting his squad leaders handle that job. They were all experienced in navigation and tactics, having been out on many patrols during numerous missions. Without a second thought, then, he often let them work on their own.

Recalling his own first solo patrol, now several months ago, Bill could empathize with his least-experienced squad leader's fear, uncertainty, and somewhat lack of confidence, when he moved out from one of their usual triangular patrol bases. The LT had instructed him to take his squad out about two hundred meters and come in on his back trail.

"Five-five, five-five, this is five-five kilo," Bruce Kubam whispered.

"This is five-five, go."

"This is five-five kilo. We're stopped here about one hundred meters out with movement to our front."

"Roger, just stay down and monitor the area. Keep me informed."

Bill was very conscious of the tension and fear Bruce was experiencing. A ground commander and his men never became accustomed to a situation like that. A few moments later he called again, still reporting movement.

"What's the direction from you?" Bill inquired.

"They're moving across our front and to the left," he replied somewhat nervously.

"Roger."

About five minutes passed when he called to tell the LT the individuals had gone by and that he wanted to follow their trail. Bill let him go, instructing him to be very careful. He had sent him out with a scout dog team that had been working with the platoon since the mission began. The dog was trained to alert on movement and scent, but could even detect a trip wire.

Scout dog teams were widely used by infantry units in Vietnam. The dog, normally a German shepherd, and its handler walked up front ahead of the point man. The dog wore a "working collar," but in no way was he leashed to his handler. It was just a means to tell the dog he was expected to do his job at that time. On the firebase, and in patrol bases, the working collar was removed and a leash was used to keep the dog from straying. Most of the dogs employed were friendly and could be petted by anyone. A few, though, were the one-owner type and it was best to leave them alone.

The dogs never barked, even if someone accidentally stepped on their feet. But the handlers could tell by their reactions if they were alerting on something. When the dog refused to move any farther something unfriendly was definitely out there. Often, though, the dogs would alert on old NDP sites, campsites, anything that still held the least trace of scent. Because of this the grunts were often checking out false alarms. The LT believed, however, it was worth the time to stop and investigate anything on which the dogs alerted. If they didn't they might regret it later.

While the men walked along, the dog would repeatedly move back and forth between the handler and the jungle to the front. On some occasions, though, the dog would lose the platoon momentarily and end up approaching the file from behind. This always scared the hell out of the trailing men. All in all, though, the LT felt more secure with the dog along.

The sad story is the fact that these dogs would never be allowed to return to the United States once having served in Vietnam. A strictly enforced health policy would keep them in Vietnam until they died.

Bruce called a short time later to tell Bill he was on his way back. Once inside the patrol base he said the fear of walking into an ambush was just too great and decided to turn back. Bill assured him he did the correct thing, complimenting him on a fine job. It was very evident this patrol had given Bruce more self-confidence, the trait so necessary for a leader to effectively handle the unexpected situations that always seem to develop.

The LT was proud of his platoon. They had come a long way since that first CA from old firebase Charles. The men were working extremely well together. Each was thoroughly familiar with the routine. He knew his job like the back of his hand, always aware of his responsibilities. It seemed Bill's job had been reduced to one of command decision making. All the normal details and duties, what they called the daily routine, were being supervised by the squad leaders.

One of the finest compliments Bill received while in the field came from the dog handler during their extraction.

"You know, LT, I've been out with many platoons and companies, but I've never felt safer at any time than I have while working with yours. You wouldn't believe some of the other companies. They're noisy as hell, even at night. They act like the gooks didn't exist."

"Well, sooner or later they're gonna pay for it," the LT replied.

"I guess so."

"Say, have you or your dog ever had a close call on patrol?"

"Yeah. My dog has been hit twice, both times when we came into a bunker complex."

"Boy, that's got to be a dedicated dog."

"I'd really feel bad if I lost him."

"Listen, I hope we can work together again soon, Jay, it's been a pleasure."

"Thanks, LT. Take care."

In Bill's mind this reflected the tremendous effort his men had made. Their actions demonstrated the truly outstanding courage, experience, unity, and morale only a seasoned, disciplined unit could project.

Their unity and integrity were tested the first week in November, however, when they met their new company commander. Captain Silver left the bush for DEROS. The men heard rumors to the effect that Captain Sharp would make some profound changes in their tactics and overall method of operation. Rumor became fact as the LTs gathered around the CO's unfolded map on the first log day to briefly discuss his operations concept.

"OK, we'll have a chance, as the days go by, to talk in detail about the company. Right now I want to go over a few things to get you on the right foot, before you move out."

Bill sat sipping a cold coke, waiting for the "bad news." The mortar crew told him to put a good word in for them because rumor had it they were going to be disbanded.

"To fight the enemy you have to work and think like they do," the new CO went on. "We're going to move two up and one back." He drew small circles and lines on his map, much like a football coach during the halftime lecture.

"How far apart will we be?" Bill asked hesitantly.

"No more than five hundred meters. Far enough so as not to constantly run into each other, but close enough so we can reinforce each other if need be."

Good idea, Bill thought, gazing at the other LTs. They also seemed to indicate their agreement.

"To use Ranger tactics we can't keep the mortar, nor can we use hammocks or take all day getting logged. We want to move all the time, so weight will be a factor we'll have to watch very closely and keep to a minimum."

He wanted the men up early in the morning and working between eight o'clock and four, ensuring they had plenty of time to set up good NDPs at night. The grunts couldn't use hammocks because they destroyed the continuity of the perimeter, vital to safety and effectiveness. In the eyes of the men, particularly the mortar crew, Captain Sharp was definitely rocking the boat. They would now find themselves carrying an M-16 on patrol rather than dropping mortar rounds in a tube from the CP.

He's right, the LT thought, walking back to his platoon area on the other side of the LZ to prepare their move. I hate to give up my hammock and the support the mortar has given us, but he's right. To be effective against the enemy, you have to employ their tactics. Despite superior firepower on the ground, in the air, and on the sea, many GIs have been killed or wounded without ever seeing an enemy soldier. The gooks know the jungle well. They have an uncanny sense of direction and can move almost undetected. Working in small numbers, they like to hit and run. They can monitor a unit indefinitely, if need be, but hit when they believe that unit to be vulnerable. Carrying an AK-47 rifle, with limited ammunition and supplies, they truly lived off the jungle. Use of trails, streams and logging roads ensured speedy, silent movement. In War Zone D speed trails were often found. These wide paths wound their way along ridges and over flat terrain, ensuring an easy, fast route for enemy couriers and combat units.

U.S. Ranger teams had great success just monitoring fresh trails. They knew from experience that Charlie rarely broke brush. So on occasion the Rangers were able to get five or six gooks in the kill zone of a claymore ambush. Needless to say, the gooks never knew what hit them when those claymores blew.

Theoretically the United States should have been employing small Ranger-type teams throughout all of South Vietnam from the beginning. The problem, in practice, is basically one of coordination and support. It would have been extremely difficult to keep track of, and resupply, so many small units. Furthermore, if a team hit something like a bunker complex, the availability of quick support with overwhelming force would present problems.

What Captain Sharp was trying to do was incorporate the tactics and strategy of a Ranger team in his platoons. How this would turn out was not certain, but one thing was obvious. The men would be doing a lot more moving than they were used to under Captain Silver.

The transition was quite smooth. Soon the platoons were operating like machines again, only this time Ranger machines. The former mortar crew was incorporated into Bill's platoon, so he had about thirty men with which to now work. This was certainly a large group when compared to the fourteen he had when he took over the platoon.

Patrolling techniques didn't change, at least it didn't seem that way. Although the men moved heavy for fifteen hundred to two thousand meters a day, they set up numerous patrol bases along the way. From these bases light patrols were sent out in the general direction of their movement. It was an efficient and effective way to search a wide area. Most importantly, it didn't physically exhaust the men.

Moving with two platoons out in front and one behind, they had to be extremely careful not to run into each other. The simple technique of "jungle commo" became a useful and frequently employed way to avoid a friendly encounter. Jungle commo was nothing more than banging a steel pot against a tree. The sound was not so loud that everyone for miles could tell where the units were, but just loud enough so that two platoons, about two hundred meters apart, could judge where they were in relation to one another.

There were times when Bill would stop and request jungle commo from the platoon moving on his side. Pointing his compass in the direction he expected it to come, the faint bang would come from a completely different location. This indicated that one or both platoon leaders were not actually where they thought they were. The LTs had to do this quite often, but it ensured that an all-American firefight would not develop due to disorientation.

The CO normally moved with the trailing platoon. The order was rotated every log day. The LTs generally preferred to be out in front, on their own, for then they didn't have to worry about enlarging their perimeter to accommodate the CP. Furthermore, they usually got a lot of criticism about their choice and shape of the NDP when the CO was with them, not to mention the noise the men made and the way they conducted their searches on light patrol. They knew too if they couldn't find a nice big tree around which the CO could set up, he would be even more critical of their choice of perimeter sites and combat techniques.

The AO remained quiet for a number of days. It wasn't until the fifth of November that activity began to escalate. On that morning the Fourth Platoon walked into an occupied bunker complex undetected, killing one gook and wounding another. A third managed to escape with the wounded individual. All three platoons closed on that complex late in the afternoon, having received word there was to be a change in mission.

17

Alpha set up a company-size NDP that night, only ninety meters from the bunker complex. An ambiguous mission change sent down from higher in the form of a map and overlay delayed their anxious movement. It was the main reason why they traveled such a short distance before setting up.

The perimeter took the shape of a triangle, with each platoon responsible for one side. The terrain seemed almost too sparse. Most of the trees were less than six inches in diameter, and even those were spaced a considerable distance apart. It made work easier, however, and by 5:30 the platoons were all locked in together. Bill had time to join the CO and the other LTs for supper. They discussed a number of subjects pertinent to the mission and general operation.

Along the perimeter, squad leaders were informing their men of the guard shift. They also checked to see that their sectors were secure. It had been a successful day for the Fourth Platoon and the company as a whole. The CO's meeting broke up when it became too dark to see anymore. The LTs moved back to their respective hootches.

It remained quiet and dry throughout the night. No one had anything significant or unusual to report at first light. By 7:30 the men were preparing to move. Some were putting gear away while others were finishing breakfast. The men seem rather slow this morning, Bill thought, swallowing the last bit of his fruit cocktail and tossing the can on the ground. The CO will be calling me over for a briefing soon, so I'd better get my stuff packed now.

The LT never got a chance to check with the CO, for as he and the grunts put away their last few pieces of equipment, the loud, sudden sound of a mortar tube broke the silence of the early morning. There was a moment's hesitation by everyone, a moment when they sort of looked at each other in disbelief. Hearts began pounding in hollow chests, for they knew there were no friendly mortar tubes in the area. That moment of hesitation soon became a fear-stricken, desperate scramble for the perimeter and what little cover could be found. The first few rounds began coming in as the LT put his helmet on and struggled to pull his rucksack over his back. He was already lying as flat as he could near one of the primary guard positions. He was next to a tree that really didn't provide much cover but psychologically seemed to help. Bill just lay there, trying to swallow, his mind seemingly blank, waiting for the rounds to impact. There was no shouting, no apparent panic, only the loud blast of each round as it exploded against the limbs of trees or the damp morning ground. Shrapnel was thrown in all directions, some of it falling like rain. In a few moments it was all over. Bill couldn't tell where the rounds fell, but none had come down on to him.

"Anybody hit, Chuck?" he nervously yelled to his first squad leader, only a few meters away. Bill's hands were shaking as he grabbed his weapon.

"I'm not sure LT," Chuck replied, quickly gazing down his sector.

The LT got up and ran down his side of the perimeter. His steel pot kept flopping down over his eyes as he ran. Farther along he found things were not OK. The second and third squads were badly hit. The rounds must have come right down my side of the perimeter, Bill thought, as medics raced from one wounded man to another. They were faced with the daunting task of trying to stop the bleeding of men with multiple shrapnel wounds. The possibility of a follow-up ground attack was the LT's next concern, so he tried to place those men who were not hit back on the perimeter. He had them push out somewhat farther to give the medics room to work.

Meanwhile, LT Beahm had shot an azimuth in the direction from which that awful sound had come. He had several of his men with grenade launchers popping rounds out in that direction. Bill sent two of his men over to join them. It was the only immediate retaliation they had available.

The CO was most likely on the radio calling for help. Bill hadn't seen him in those first few moments when all hell broke loose. He now only saw the scurrying of men in every direction, almost like ants when someone has disturbed their nest.

"LT, one of your men is in bad shape," a member of the Second Platoon said, as Bill gazed around, trying to figure out what he needed to do next. Without a reply, he followed the pointing finger and hurried over to find all three medics working on Dennis Debickero, one of his assistant gunners. One held an IV (intravenous injection) running to his arm, another was putting pressure on his chest, while a third performed mouth-to-mouth resuscitation. Bill got down on one knee and could do nothing but pray. Dennis had lost all his color and now made only faint groaning sounds. Moments later Bill's AG died. Shrapnel from one of the mortar rounds had pierced his neck and taken his life in the process.

The medics immediately began to cry, as if it were their fault that he died. Somehow the LT's emotions didn't dominate his thoughts and he was able to assure them there was nothing more anyone could have done to have saved Dennis. The medics were now needed by the men who could still be helped. Bill rose to his feet as a poncho liner was draped over the body. He scurried down the perimeter once again, trying to help those who were wounded and ensuring that security was adequate. Blood, bandages, rucksacks, and weapons were scattered all around. The gooks would occasionally hit a unit after such an attack so this continued to worry the LT. Maybe there were just too few of them to mount a ground attack, he thought.

LT Beahm and his men secured an area adjacent to the perimeter when word was received the medevac birds were on their way. It was time, in all the confusion and disarray, to determine who was injured and how badly. The pilots would want that information to make sure the most serious got out first.

Sergeant Treadway, the CO's field first sergeant, did an outstanding job organizing the medevac. He had to get all the injured out on rigid litters and JPs, for there was no place the birds could sit down. Instead, they had to hover overhead, sitting ducks for any gooks still around. The noise from each bird was so loud it seemed necessary for Sergeant Treadway to yell into the handset to give instructions to the pilots. In all there were thirteen casualties. One was killed and two were seriously wounded. Eleven of Bill's men were among the casualties, along with two from the Second Platoon.

Yesterday Alpha ruled with the upper hand, but this morning Charlie took his revenge and really did a fine job in the process. It was apparent, in Bill's mind anyway, that Charlie must have probed their position during the night, calculating the direction and distance from his mortar tube. Otherwise, the gooks were generally not that accurate with indirect fire.

The grunts found few impact craters, indicating that most of the rounds exploded over their heads. Since no one in the Fourth Platoon was hit, and only two in the Second Platoon, it was obvious most of the rounds did come right in on Bill's side of the perimeter.

In what was, without a doubt, the most courageous act Bill had seen during his tour, LT Beahm and volunteers from his platoon ventured back into the bunker complex shortly after the medevac. They had to retrieve an alpha alpha (automatic ambush) set up the evening before. Beahm initially directed a loach over the ambush site, hoping its vibration and static electricity would set off the battery-operated claymores. It was to no avail, however, and he finally had to move in and manually disarm it. Brigade policy would not allow such a booby trap to be left behind. It had to be either picked up or destroyed in place. Dick chose to do the former, and accomplished the tense, nerve-racking job with precision, safely returning to the company perimeter a short time later. On the LT's return the company pulled back six hundred meters to the north. Filling their canteens at a small stream, the men listened as jets pounded the bunker complex with five-hundred-pound bombs.

In terms of numbers, the company was still tactically operative. After that experience, however, the men were mentally, emotionally and psychologically ineffective. Battalion had them scheduled for extraction the next day, but this meant having to spend another night and morning in the bush, hounded by the terrible fear and anxiety of a possible repeat performance. The CO ordered the company split into two groups. Bill set up with the Fourth Platoon while the Second Platoon and CP NDP'd about five hundred meters to the east. The LT stressed that noise discipline was extremely critical. It was also important to refrain from putting up hootches until just before dark. Everyone cooperated fully with the instructions.

It was a dark, dreadful night, one where the imagination pictured many things, all difficult to call real or unreal. Bill was awakened at first light and stood guard with one of his men. They had decided to double the guard shift to help calm unsteady nerves. Not too long after Bill's shift began both men saw something in the faint light darting away from the perimeter and into the dark jungle. The shadow, they both thought, may have been that of a human. The LT didn't know whether it was disbelief or the fear of causing panic, but neither man made any attempt to fire at the figure moving before them. Bill began to think they were being probed again.

As the morning light seeped into the NDP, Bill could sense the absolute and utter fear the men had of getting hit again. He felt the same way. He couldn't recall ever being so afraid in his life. After he and LT Mitchell conferred, they decided to pick up and move immediately, even if was just one hundred meters. As long as the gooks couldn't keep a firm fix on their location they could feel a little more secure. Doing just that, the men relocated one hundred meters south of the LZ from which they were scheduled to extract.

At nine o'clock they moved up to the LZ and got it quickly secured. Shortly thereafter the rest of the company arrived. It wasn't long before Yellow One came in to pick them up. Bill's only thought, as he was lifted out of the jungle that morning, was the overriding fear of having to return to that same area again. The mission was over, but the memory of that morning and the eerie, frightening sound of the enemy mortar would, without a doubt, remain with him for the rest of his life.

18

The two main hospitals serving Military Region Three (MR3) were located in Long Binh and Saigon. It was to these hospitals that Alpha's wounded men were sent.

The hospital at Long Binh was comprised of many wards and several administration buildings. Each was nothing more than a Quonset hut with a rough, crude exterior. The interiors, however, were very modern, with all the latest in medical equipment and technology available. In Saigon, the hospital was more like those we see back in the world. Everything was contained in one large building, several stories high.

Once the company arrived at Mace, following their extraction, Bill boarded a truck convoy that made a daily run to Bien Hoa. It was his first visit to the rear since the CA from Charles on the fourteenth of August. The next day he was driven to both hospitals where he spent the entire day visiting his men.

Bill thought he had seen what the tragedy of war was like when his platoon returned to firebase Charles and came upon the VC bodies and when he saw his AG die in the bush. But never did the fact hit so hard as it did when he visited these hospitals. To see men with missing limbs, suffering internal wounds and severe burns, he really wanted to cry. These were men maimed by a war they didn't understand and certainly couldn't call their own. They lay in beds wondering why they had to be the ones to suffer. If the leaders of the nations involved in this struggle had taken a walk through the wards at Long Binh and Saigon, maybe they would have ended this senseless thing years before.

What a sad situation, Bill thought. The American soldier has to die or be maimed in a country as close to his heart as the distance he was from his loved ones at home. He has to fight for a people who have known war and suffering all their lives, people who have somehow made the adjustment, regardless. He has to die or be maimed for a people who plow their fields, tend to their rice paddies, and raise a family, all within the sights and sounds of war and political struggle. These people have only one desire, and that is to be left alone. Their hope is to continue in the traditional lifestyle of their forefathers. Would the lives, customs, traditions, and interests of these people, based on myriad past generations, change any, if at all, whether there existed a democratic or communist form of government in Vietnam? Bill seriously doubted it, and this made him sick when he thought of the young Americans who were being killed and wounded here. And this was just a few of the hundreds of thousands of others who had fallen to a soil that has remained unchanged over centuries of different rule.

He really felt sorry for these young guys, for many would never fully recover from their wounds. Instead, they would have to go through life with one limb, one eye, a speech impediment, or with the limp of an old man. And these were the lucky ones. Others would suffer from what is now known as post-traumatic stress syndrome and be haunted by this war for the rest of their lives.

Bill often thought about the possibility of being wounded. He thought he'd rather die than to lose his eyes or limbs. Somehow, though, judging from the men he saw, the strong will to live always seems to prevail. Most of the permanently disabled were already beginning the mental adjustment they would have to make when returned to society and friends at home.

Despite their pain, his men were in good spirits. Several had plastic tubes running from their noses and mouths so they had difficulty speaking, but their eyes were bright and alert. Bill told each one about the last day of the fateful mission and what their buddies now on the firebase were doing. While they enjoyed hearing the news, the LT could tell too that deep inside they had seen enough of the war and now wanted only to go home. Most were to get their wish, for hospital officials told Bill if he got three back for field duty he would be lucky. Time passed very quickly that day, but he assured the men they would receive visitors as often as possible, bringing them news from the field and mail from home.

The LT and his driver passed through many streets of downtown Saigon as they made their way back to Bien Hoa. Never before had Bill seen such congestion. Cars, scooters, Lambrettas, bicycles and pedestrians were everywhere and going in every direction. It took a skilled and extremely patient driver to navigate the streets of that city. Much of it was reminiscent of Vung Tau, with its crude, crowded shops and homes built right on the edge of the narrow streets. Other sections of Saigon, however, were quite modern, with many large administrative buildings and beautiful temples. Guards patrolled many of these buildings, some of which had the familiar concertina wire placed along the outer walls.

Crossing the Saigon River bridge, Bill could see American and Vietnamese supply ships, tied along the docks, being unloaded. He wondered, as they passed bunker positions along the roadway, how much of those supplies would end up in VC and NVA hands.

He returned to the firebase the following day and learned that a memorial service was planned for his assistant gunner. Bill discussed the service with the chaplain because he suggested the LT deliver a brief eulogy as part of the service. Bill spent the entire night thinking of what to say. He had never been asked to do anything of that kind before.

The next morning the men gathered in a small wooden chapel. It was barely large enough to hold members of the Third Platoon let alone representatives from the company and battalion. Midway through the short service Bill stood up and began to speak. In a trembling, almost choking voice, he said that on the sixth of November they had lost an American soldier. For members of Alpha Company and the Third Platoon, he was a close friend. The LT recalled all the friendships Dennis had made, the determination and professional attitude he had shown in everything he did. Bill said he hoped these attributes would carry over into their own hearts and minds, and his men would continue to approach their jobs with the same attributes Dennis exemplified so well.

Following the benediction, the men filed out of the chapel and went back to the details that awaited them. Bill had been placed in many difficult situations since the first CA, but none was more difficult than standing before the men that morning. He was mentally relieved when the service was concluded, but felt they had paid a fine tribute to a most deserving soldier.

The men all earned their CIBs (Combat Infantryman Badge) that fateful November morning. But more than that it instilled in everyone's mind how careful they would have to be on future missions. None of the men were particularly anxious to receive a Purple Heart if they could help it. Until the sixth of November they had not come face-to-face with death, even though on several occasions it was close at hand. The grunts now realized that Charlie meant business. He wasn't just fooling around.

Bill often asked himself why he continued to do his job and encourage his men in theirs, when he could see the useless, aimless results of their efforts. He was just afraid to buck the system, afraid his future would be jeopardized. He wondered, though, if his attitude would have changed had he been one of the wounded.

There were many nights following the mortar attack when the LT lay awake, recalling that morning and how lucky he was. Everything they did, everything that happened to them, was simply a matter of chance or luck. The afternoon the Third Platoon ran into the URS site and captured the radios. Had they been a few meters off, to the left or the right, they would never have seen the place. The day Torres captured the POW. Had they been a little earlier or a little later, they would never have crossed paths with those individuals. Had Bill decided to set up his hootch in a different location on the evening of November 5, he might not be alive today.

It seemed their lives were truly in the hands of God. There was no way to change or control their destiny. Bill recalled how Tom, the former XO, asked God for help when he had to make difficult decisions. He now found himself doing the same thing. Many of the men believed there was always someone with them, watching over them, just as it says in the fourth verse of the Twenty-third Psalm:

> Yea, though I walk through the valley of the shadow
> of death, I will fear no evil: for thou art with me;
> thy rod and thy staff they comfort me.

Bill lay in his hootch each night praying to God for the safety of his men, his family's health, and an end to this and all future wars. He now held a greater belief in the existence of God than at any other time in his life.

19

It wasn't long before the men were in the bush again, beginning a mission scheduled for eleven days. This represented a reduction from the normal fifteen- and sixteen-day ordeals. The grunts certainly had no complaints.

Patrolling for three days, they found little evidence of enemy activity in the area. The latter half of the third day was a concentrated effort to locate an LZ. They were scheduled to get logged the following day and had to close on an adequate pad.

Log days were always looked upon with favor and a slight sense of excitement by the men. It usually meant mail from home, a hot meal, and clean clothes. The problem, however, was that the heightened anticipation of the log and the accompanying party atmosphere during its operation produced a lower sense of awareness of one's surroundings. Consequently, it was a security risk to all involved. On some occasions they even had to bypass certain basic security measures due to bad terrain or insufficient time. This brought the lack of security down to a dangerous level.

In most instances the LZ chosen was a one-shipper and security capability was 360 degrees. Each platoon was given a sector to cover, normally designated by superimposing a clock on the LZ or defining them with prominent terrain features. Ideally each position had visual contact with the one to its immediate left and right, but this was not always possible. Hence the placement of claymore mines out in front was all the more important.

The CP normally set up with the platoon having the most accessible avenue to the LZ, for supplies were hand carried to one main distribution point. From this one location each platoon received its issue of food, water, and combat equipment. A hot chow line was usually set up in this area also. The men were required to pass through the line wearing their steel pot and carrying a weapon. While not always adhered to, this company policy was a means to maintain security and safety.

"Log bird's inbound," yelled one of the RTO's in the CP.

"OK, pop smoke."

Alpha normally had one grunt out on the pad. His job was to pop smoke for the chopper pilots and to help unload the birds once they landed. The pop of the smoke grenade was quite loud. If you weren't expecting it, you could mistake it for a rifle shot.

"Log bird, log bird, Tiger three-one, over."

"Log bird."

"Roger, Tiger three-one, smoke's out."

"Thank you."

It was difficult for the pilots to spot the smoke, especially when they were still pretty high in the air. The smoke seemed to filter up through the trees at a slow rate.

"Tiger three-one, log bird."

"Tiger three-one, go."

"Roger, I got goofy grape, over."

"That's most affirm, come on down."

Once the pilots identify the smoke and the color is confirmed, they begin their descent and make a final approach. Smoke is put out continuously so they have a firm fix on the LZ at all times.

The first load of supplies to come in is usually clean clothes and cold sodas. It seemed the men took the most time changing clothes and backlogging the dirty stuff. The cold Cokes were the incentive to make the change a quick one. Inevitably there was always one platoon that came out short in terms of clean clothes. The men rarely got the correct sizes but this didn't create too much static. As long as they had something clean to wear it didn't matter whether the pants looked more like Bermuda shorts. When the men arrived in country they were given five new sets of fatigues, all of which fit very well. Funny, though, that was the last they normally saw of them.

Very often the XO and mail clerk would also be on the first sortie of the log bird. The clerk brought the company mail but he wasn't allowed to distribute it until the men finished packing their rucksacks. This was a wise policy, for if he gave the mail out first nothing else would get done. The XO would report to the CO on various administrative matters. His basic responsibility in the rear was to represent the CO when the captain was in the bush. The XO was usually the most senior LT in the company, in most cases having spent the first six to eight months in the bush as a platoon leader.

By the time everyone had changed clothes the log bird was making its second or third sortie. On these runs C-rations and water were the main cargo. If there were any personnel coming out to the bush from the firebase they too were usually aboard. Similarly, if anyone was scheduled to go in, he normally hopped aboard one of the return flights. Turnaround time depended on how far the company was from the firebase, but an average round trip was made in about thirty minutes.

Log day was, without a doubt, a most difficult one for the platoon sergeants and squad leaders. They were responsible for the receipt and distribution of all the supplies. They normally had little time to even enjoy a cold Coke or the hot meal. Furthermore, they had to absorb all the criticism from the men when items they had ordered were not received.

By early afternoon the men had everything they were going to carry packed away in their rucks. It was often a problem trying to find space for the food they wanted to carry, especially if they had received a package of goodies from home. Bill recalled one previous log day when one of his men received an huge salami and several other packages besides. George Shimabuku ended up backlogging most of it, hoping it would not be spoiled by the time he got back to the firebase.

With the few remaining backlog items on the LZ waiting for the last sortie of the bird, the platoon sergeants and squad leaders would make last-minute checks of their men and areas, ensuring that everything received was distributed correctly and their sectors were free of trash. Sumps, dug earlier in the morning, provided central areas for the burning of trash. By termination of the log these holes were filled to the brim with food cartons, package wrappings, unwanted cans of food and other scraps of paper and wood. They tried to ensure cans of food were opened before being thrown away to prevent Charlie from getting hold of it or having the cans explode in the hot fire.

While the platoon sergeants made last-minute checks, the LTs were getting briefed by the CO on the next phase of the mission. The two platoons that would work out in front naturally had to move out before the CP and remaining platoon did. They always tried to move at least five hundred meters from the LZ if they could, but with heavy rucks it was always a struggle.

The LTs were briefing their squad leaders on the new mission as the log bird came in on its final run. It was just about time to move out once again. Only the crackling of the burn piles could be heard as they slowly made their way through the thick brush. Every once in a while a faint bang would be heard, indicating that someone forgot to open a can he threw away back at the LZ.

The men began struggling after only two hundred fifty meters due to the rough terrain and the weight of ten quarts of water, claymore mine, trip flare, smoke grenades, steel pot, and weapon. It was on these occasions that the point man wished he was at the end of the file and not the front.

On this particular log day Bill's platoon and LT Beahm's Second were out in front. The CO expected them to move at least four hundred fifty meters, giving the CP a chance to move a safe distance off the LZ before having to set up for the night. Bill managed to travel four hundred meters before it got too late. Quickly setting up the NDP, he called in his location and received grid coordinates from the other platoons. Beahm had traveled a little farther than Bill while the CP and the Fourth Platoon managed only two hundred meters.

A cold rain fell off and on over the next several days, making everything the grunts did seem like a major effort. Their patrolling had turned up no evidence of Charlie so it seemed they were just wasting their time. The next afternoon Bill decided it was time to set up a patrol base after having moved heavy for approximately four hundred meters.

"Torres! Let's stop here and set up a papa bravo."

Reynaldo Torres was walking point for his squad as usual. Bill rotated the three squads on a daily basis so each was point squad every third day. It was the only fair way to do it.

"Where do you want my men, LT?"

"Put your squad between that big black tree and the one that's leaning over, OK?"

"Roger."

As the men in the third squad filed by, the LT and his RTO tried to find a logical place to put his first and second squads.

"TJ, we're setting up here for a while. Put your people in over here. Link up with Torrres on your right and put your gun on that trail."

Each squad carried a machine gun and the LT tried his best to put them in strategic locations. Chuck Holtz's squad was the trailing one that day and, when he finally passed by, Bill told him to fill in between Torres and TJ. He wanted the trailing gun to cover their back trail.

Slipping off his ruck and letting it fall to the ground, Bill pulled out his map and began calculating their location.

"Hey, Dayton, what'd you get for a pace?"

"Uh, I think it was 405, LT."

"Thanks."

Dayton Stout was the best pace man Bill had so he normally took the figure he gave him as the true distance traveled. Measuring off the distance on their azimuth, the LT came up with a six-digit grid coordinate for their location.

"Mike, call that in. It's close enough for government work."

The head RTO was in the process of putting up his long whip antenna. It was used in patrol bases and NDPs because it provided the best transmission and reception quality. The short whip had a very limited range but was essential when moving through thick brush. Mike Kampen took the LT's acetate map on which Bill had written the grid figures. Once Kampen shacked the numbers, he called the CP some six hundred meters away.

"Four-three, four-three, two-four tango, over."

"Four-three, go ahead."

"Roger, two-four tango, we're in papa bravo status at this time and I have our location. Are you prepared to copy, over?"

"Roger, send it."

"I set delta foxtrot, I shack kilo alpha Zulu bravo November alpha, for a magic magic of echo golf, how copy, over?"

"Roger, set delta foxtrot, shack kilo alpha Zulu bravo November alpha, for a magic magic of echo golf, over."

"Roger, solid copy."

"Thanks much. I got negative further."

"Negative further, out."

No sooner had Mike handed Bill the map when an M-16 fired full clip on automatic. The LT dove for the ground as men hit the deck around him. Other men began firing too, which scared Bill, for some of his men were still outside the perimeter running out their claymores. As they came dashing through the heavy brush the LT crawled over to the edge of the perimeter from where the firing began. By this time all was quiet again.

"TJ, what happened?" the LT asked nervously.

"Two gooks walked up on me while I was putting out my claymore." TJ was breathing hard, having just gotten back inside the perimeter. "I think they thought I was a gook too, LT. We just sort of looked at each other for a moment before I opened up on them."

"We're they NVA? Could you tell?"

"I think so, and I hit one bad too."

"OK, TJ, get your radio and three or four men. We'll go out and see what we can find. Mike, call Charlie Oscar and tell him we spotted two gooks, possibly NVA, and we're going out to track them down."

"Got a solid," responded Kampen.

"Chuck, Torres, make sure you got all your people accounted for and on the perimeter. You'll have to move a few of your men over to cover for TJ while we're out."

In a few moments the tracking party was put together and moved to the initial contact site. It took about twenty minutes to find a blood trail. Judging from the amount of blood they found and its location on the vegetation, it was obvious TJ had hit one bad. It was most likely a hip or stomach wound. They found and followed the broken brush trail for a while before turning around. Bill didn't want to go too far with only five men. Upon returning to the perimeter the CO called and asked if Bill wanted the Pink Team. The LT decided it was better to organize a larger patrol.

Picking up the trail once again, they followed it for two hundred meters without finding anyone. The individual was definitely losing a lot of blood, though. The LT wished he had a dog team along on this mission. About fifty meters farther they came upon a tree where bandage wrappings and lots more blood were found. They could only see one distinct set of boot prints leading up to the tree so the wounded gook must have been carried by the other. Continuing on a little more, they failed to find anyone. The medic said they could figure the gook was a step-on based on the amount of blood he lost. A little frustrated, the patrol turned around and headed back.

Bill spoke to TJ again before calling in a final sit rep. The gooks could very well have mistaken him for one of their own since he was a dark Mexican-American. That moment of indecision on their part probably saved TJ's life. In any event, what the LT wasn't aware of was the fact that TJ dove behind a log after firing his weapon and called for direct fire over his head. He hoped his men would hit the gooks too, stopping them in their tracks for sure. Bill hadn't realized either, that AK fire from the gooks came through the perimeter during the initial encounter. The men were quick to mention this, for it meant receipt of a CIB for those who hadn't yet been awarded one.

The Combat Infantryman's Badge was probably one of the most cherished medals the grunts received while in Vietnam. It represented courage under fire, a challenge to death and injury, a true sacrifice of one's heart and soul.

The company was extracted from the bush several days later. When they got back to Mace, Bill began writing down an account of the contact. He planned to recommend TJ for a Bronze Star with V, a medal given for valor, based on meritorious action in combat. His alert, intelligent reactions, along with his courage and disregard for his own life, gave him a medically confirmed step-on. Thankfully there was no injury to friendly troops either. In Bill's mind no one was more deserving of the medal. Ever since that rainy evening on old firebase Sherman, when the colonel walked among a proud group of men, personally awarding medals for actions in the bush, Bill vowed he would do the same. He wanted his men to not only be recognized by medals, but also through promotions. Theirs was a thankless job. No pay scale was truly representative of the sacrifice they were making, but the LT wanted to ensure they were getting everything they could possibly receive.

Alpha Company was extracted on 21 November and Bill's platoon arrived at Firebase Hall around 9:30 a.m. The men had a chance to get cleaned up as best they could and even played a little football inside the perimeter. A light rain and a cool breeze made the next morning extremely raw. An awards ceremony was held later in the day, which helped warm things up. Purple Hearts and CIBs were awarded for previous contacts. After the ceremony Captain Sharp told his platoon leaders a new LT, Johnny Cook, was now assigned to Alpha. Sharp wanted Cook to walk with each platoon on the next mission. This would give him a chance to learn company policy and observe tactics. He would switch platoons on each log day.

Bill took the opportunity on the following day to travel to Saigon to visit his men in the hospital. He learned that several had already been flown back to the world. The LT returned to Hall the next day.

On November 25 Alpha celebrated Thanksgiving with a huge dinner at midday but later made a CA into the bush once again. Over the next several days all three platoons discovered bunker complexes and these were subsequently destroyed. Bravo Company, operating to the south, had several contacts with Charlie. They called in air support initially and later requested artillery fire. The rounds flew over Bill's platoon as they whizzed south to hit a bunker complex.

On December 2, Alpha Company got resupplied again. Bill got two new men and he assigned them to Torres' squad. Bravo Company and the Blues were still encountering Charlie to the south. Word came through that a low bird went down in Bravo's AO.

Over the next several days Alpha Company found numerous trails but nothing more. LT Cook was now walking with the Third Platoon to observe operations. Patrolling of the area continued until December 8, when they were extracted and flown back to Mace.

Vung Tau had arrived once again. It felt good to sleep late, play Frisbee and swim in the ocean. The men also took the opportunity to write letters home. The Third Platoon scheduled a dinner at Cyrano's Restaurant followed by a party at the Palace Hotel. As usual the three days went by very quickly and on December 12 Alpha flew back to Mace.

20

There were really no holidays or vacations for the grunts in Vietnam. Every day seemed alike. The only way Alpha Company knew it was Monday was when the medics handed the men a large, orange malaria pill, taken weekly.

Alpha's mission, which began on December 13, was scheduled for two weeks. The men didn't know whether they would be in the bush the entire time or possibly get extracted before Christmas. It would be based solely on activity in the AO and the tactical situation at the time.

The weather on the morning of the thirteenth was sunny and warm, but Bill didn't appreciate the warmth because he had just learned the rear job he was hoping for didn't come through. He would now be out in the bush until early February.

Yellow One was right on time and by 9:00 a.m. the men were back in the bush. Bill moved his platoon about seventy-five meters off the LZ before stopping to wait for a dog team that was assigned to him for the mission. The terrain was very thick with lots of bamboo. Once the dog team arrived he moved heavy again for about five hundred meters and proceeded to set up an NDP. The next morning was clear and the Third Platoon continued to patrol the area with negative results. A day later Bill realized they would soon need more drinking water and called in that request. They moved heavy again before setting up a patrol base to await the kick out of water. With the lack of activity in the AO the men took the opportunity to do a lot of reading and writing in the patrol bases. Some made their own Christmas cards expressing, in words and pictures, their thoughts and prayers, this at a time when there was no peace on earth or good will toward men. Security was always maintained, for that was utmost on their mind, no matter what day of the year it happened to be. Christmas and New Year cease fires were considered fictitious. In fact, the men thought the gooks were more intent on contact during those particular days.

Thoughts expressed on these cards were pretty much directed to friends and loved ones at home. Most of the men had always spent Christmas with their families. This year, however, they found themselves nine thousand miles away in a strange land. Chuck Holtz wrote cards to his relatives and friends, his thoughts brought to life through poetry. "A Soldier's Daydream," which he wrote on December 18, summarized very well the feelings and emotions characteristic of all infantry soldiers in a combat zone. It read as follows:

> In the life of a soldier every day there's a time
> When just for a moment home dwells on his mind.
> Not the houses, the streets, or the car that he drives,
> But the loved ones he's missing and their everyday lives.
> His craving warm love that's waiting for him

And just for a second he's back home again.
Then a shot and a cry of frenzied confusion
And the young soldier wakes from his warm loves illusion
The world for a time is a torrent and blare
And then in hushed silence smoke clears from the air.
The danger is past and all threat gone away
But before thoughts return the young soldier must pray.
Dear God, I'm a soldier so far from my home
And though you are with me I still feel alone.
So if fighting for freedom is what I must do,
I'll pray every day and ask one thing of you.
In each day of my life please reserve me some time
For thoughts of my loved ones to dwell on my mind.

It was raining very little these days. Most nights were clear and cold, with millions of stars covering the black sky. The dry season had at last arrived. Each night, as darkness set in on the grunts, they did nothing but hit the sack. Only the three guards on first shift remained awake. Noise and light discipline on the whole were good. Only occasionally did they have a problem with someone snoring or accidentally tripping a flare. Bill often lay awake in his hootch for hours after it got dark, looking up at the moon and stars, thinking about the men's accomplishments and weak points, trying to guess what the coming months would bring. He would usually fall asleep with these thoughts and wake to the soft voice of one of his men telling him it was his turn for guard. There were times, however, when he had nightmares. He would dream they were being overrun. Suddenly waking up, his eyes a picture of fear, he would find everything quiet except for the occasional chirp of a bird or the sound of a cricket breaking the stillness of the surrounding jungle. There were times too when he woke up in the middle of the night thinking all his men had been killed and he was left to wake to that horrible sight. A rustle from one of the guard positions or the sound of someone turning over on his air mattress brought the LT back to reality. He would fall back to sleep once again.

During this mission Bill had a chance to talk to the CO about the remainder of his tour. Captain Sharp said he could take R&R in early February and then take over an XO position in Bien Hoa. This meant the LT had two more missions after this current one. At least now Bill had an end in sight. This, of course, was contingent upon Alpha getting another LT by then. Sharp had decided to assign LT Cook to the Fourth Platoon and was sending LT Mitchell to the rear for some unknown reason. He thus needed one more LT to replace Bill.

The days seemed to pass very quickly and soon it was Christmas Eve. The patrolling had failed to find anything or anyone. Because of this, battalion gave Alpha Company word they would be on the firebase for Christmas. Morale of the men jumped 200 percent when this news was received. The Third Platoon demonstrated their excitement by cutting a Christmas tree from among the inexhaustible supply around them. Decorating it with assorted cans, LRRP bags and paper, it was quite a sight. C-ration cans of fruit were poured into a large container making a delicious fruit salad. A ham, sent from home and carried the entire mission by Chuck Holtz, was cooked that evening. Hard candy, also sent from home, was offered to all by Dave Moore, as he walked along the perimeter with his bag of goodies. Someone had to play the part of Santa! During the festivities a prayer for peace was offered, each man asking for a conscious effort by his fellow man to end this and all wars.

It happened to rain later that night, even though they were now in the dry season. Bill didn't even bother to put up his poncho, but slept as best he could to the light rain falling on the leaves, his face and body. Who cares, he thought, tomorrow's extraction. We're going back to the firebase for Christmas! Somehow this Christmas meant more to Bill than any he could recall at home. The men had brought the real meaning of Christmas to the jungles of Vietnam, absent all the trivia normally associated with the holidays back in the world.

Mace was crowded this holiday weekend. It seemed most of the battalion companies were on the firebase. The LT got to choose eleven of his men to go back to Bien Hoa to attend Bob Hope's Christmas show. Colonel Hodges called a battalion formation in the afternoon to speak about holiday safety. He also announced that we would be moving our AO farther west on subsequent missions.

21

Sure enough, with the New Year came word the battalion would be moving. This, of course, was something the men had become accustomed to through the course of their tours. The move reflected the continued withdrawal of U.S. combat forces toward the population centers of Bien Hoa, Long Binh, and Saigon. The men hoped, one day soon, it would be a withdrawal home.

On January 2 Alpha was in the bush again. Thick brush was making movement very difficult. Light patrols were sent out throughout the day with negative results. The next morning Bill's platoon got a jolt when Bob Freeman accidentally fired his weapon while he was cleaning it. Luckily no one was hurt. All three platoons moved heavy for a while and then set up patrol bases from which they did light recons. The Third Platoon was with the CP during this time. Bill enjoyed the evening bullshit sessions he had with the CO. Captain Sharp was funny as hell and sure could talk up a storm. The LT also enjoyed philosophizing with Chuck Holtz about anything and everything. When Bill sent Chuck and Don Lloyd in for DEROS on January 4 he felt it was an end of an era for him. These guys were seasoned veterans which, in turn, provided Bill with a lot of confidence during their time in the bush. With their departure, the LT found he was beginning to get a little shaky, especially since he now had the responsibility of more and more men, men who had little or no experience in the bush.

The next morning Bill had to medevac one of his new men because he had been taking drugs in the rear and was now having withdrawal symptoms. He had come from a company operating to the north and was obviously being passed from one company to another.

After another in a series of wet nights and cool mornings, Bill linked up with the other platoons and they all pushed off to the northwest. Later that afternoon the LT got word that LT Beahm had wrenched his knee and had to be medevaced. The light patrols Bill had sent out reported finding many bunkers. Late in the afternoon they got a real scare when a Pink Team working in that area to the northwest reconned by fire without notifying anyone. When things settled down that evening Bill decided to have Captain Sharp move to his location the next day so the LT could show him the bunker complex and let him blow it up.

Just before dawn the next day, after a relatively quiet and dry night, the CO called Bill to say intelligence reported gooks in the open north of the nearby mountain Nui Chau Chan. However, after a short time it was concluded that what they were really seeing were lightning bugs. The LT just shook his head on that one.

Once Captain Sharp reached Bill's platoon they sat down and waited for the engineers. They arrived a short time later with twelve cratering charges and proceeded to blow up the bunkers. LT Beahm was now back in the bush too. The next morning all the platoons linked up for log day. Bill took a light patrol out during the log and found another set of bunkers. They also discovered that three of the charges from yesterday didn't blow. The LT requested wire and detonators and finished the job. When the patrol got back to the LZ, Bill was disappointed to find that his platoon sergeant and squad leaders hadn't set aside food, water, and clothes for him and the men on patrol. Otherwise, the log was smooth.

The next morning was cloudy and cool. Bill moved his platoon out heavy for two hundred fifty meters before taking a break. He had two dog teams with him. Unfortunately, a short time later the dogs got into a fight with one another and both had to be medevaced. The rest of the company continued on as Bill stayed behind to provide security for the medevac bird. Once this was done he moved heavy again for quite a distance before taking another break. The company had moved a considerable distance and it was hard for the Third Platoon to catch up. They all ended up traveling a total of thirty-five hundred meters that day. The following day was no easier. They traveled a total of forty-one hundred meters and had to NDP in a lousy bamboo grove. Morale was rapidly deteriorating.

On January 11, the LT was instructed to secure a log site for Alpha's resupply. The men of Alpha were told they would be moving onto the new firebase, Cross Sabers, on January 13 to help in its construction. Two platoons, the Second and Third, would stay at Sabers while the Fourth would occupy a nearby hill.

Walking onto the partially completed firebase following the eleven-day mission, the grunts were tired but happy to be out of the bush. They had traveled over six klicks the previous two days to be in a blocking position just south of the firebase. The secretary of the Army had been scheduled to arrive at Sabers on the twelfth for a tour of the soon-to-be model firebase. Alpha's mission these last two days was to merely occupy the mortar belt surrounding the base, running light patrols in the area, essentially keeping Charlie from using his mortar tube while the secretary was touring. Funny thing, the secretary never showed up so the cross-country marathon was nothing but a total waste of energy. However, the men were told they wouldn't have to CA again until after Vung Tau, which was scheduled for January 27. This produced many happy smiles, even though the men knew the next twelve days would be nothing but hard labor.

That it was, for while most of the heavy work had already been completed, there were thousands of sandbags to fill and lay, wire to be strung, and countless other odds and ends to attend to. They were literally driven into the ground those first few days, for the work day began at seven o'clock in the morning and didn't end until it got too dark to see anymore. After several days of this nonsense the LTs convinced the CO who, in turn, convinced the colonel, that they could probably get more work done working an eight-to-five shift. The men were just too tired to continue that slave schedule.

On the evening of January 16, LT Beahm was walking across the dark firebase when he unknowingly fell into an ammunition storage pit. He injured both legs badly in the fall. The next morning he was transported to the hospital in Long Binh where they had to put casts on both legs. Needless to say, Beahm did not return to the bush after that. Staff

Sergeant Lyn Harrand took over the Second Platoon in the interim.

As the days passed, and the trip to Vung Tau got closer, the men became less and less enthusiastic about doing the construction work. The job, nevertheless, was getting done. Sandbagged hootches not only provided protection but were built like brickwork. They were thus as eye appealing as they were secure. This was true of every building on the firebase, including the bunkers. If buildings were not put up correctly they were immediately torn down and redone. Some of them were torn down several times before being built correctly.

The morning of the twenty-seventh finally arrived, not a minute too soon as far as the men were concerned. Just as before, they traveled by Chinook to Xuan Loc, conversed with the Vietnamese people at the airfield, and then were flown the rest of the way by fixed wing. This was to be Bill's last trip to the ocean city, for he was scheduled to DEROS before Alpha's turn came up again. The highlight of his entire tour came on the first evening when the CP and the LT's men held a dinner in his honor at Cyrano's Restaurant and presented him with a Cav watch. All he could say was thanks, for there were no words to express the feelings he deeply held for them.

Like all the other trips to Vung Tau, the time went by too quickly. The men had to forget about the Palace, the Mai Linh, the beach, and those pretty girls and start focusing on the new mission. They actually looked forward to the bush this time, for there was still a great deal of work to be done at Sabers and they had had enough of that for a while.

Replacements had been coming in at a constant rate since the first of the year. For once Bill would be taking more than thirty men to the bush. While it could be said there is security in numbers, he really didn't want this many men in his platoon. According to the Army manual, an infantry platoon is supposed to number forty-three men. But in the context of a guerrilla war like Vietnam, where speed, silence, and control are essential, anything over twenty becomes difficult to handle. This was to be Bill's last four days in the jungles of Vietnam. His replacement, LT Bill Herzer, had arrived and Bill's R&R to Bangkok was confirmed for February 7. The LT was extremely apprehensive about going out on the mission, even though he would be out for only four days. The CO, however, wanted Bill to acquaint LT Herzer and LT Jerry Sidio, Beahm's replacement, with their method of operation. There was nothing Bill could do but make the CA and hope for the best. He now knew how John Gonzales felt, deep inside, that day months ago, being so short, when anything but the bush became his only desire.

With so many men control was going to be a major problem. Furthermore, the inexperience of the new people would present other problems, particularly if they had the bad luck of becoming involved in a contact. Intelligence reports indicated an increase of enemy activity within the AO, so the LT was not too optimistic about having a quiet mission.

Yellow One inserted the company as usual and, for the first day and a half, they didn't see much of anything. Bill was pleased to see that his new people were adapting to their environment very well. Noise and light discipline was good the first night and they weren't complaining at all about the humping. When they were moving, though, the file was spread out over a long distance, making coordination extremely difficult. The LT could recall, with twenty men, how he used to move out heavy from a patrol base for about two hundred meters and then take a five-minute break. Hell, if he had done that now he'd still have guys standing in the perimeter. Construction of the patrol bases took quite a bit longer now too. It was certainly longer than Bill desired. If there was any time when Charlie liked to hit a unit it was when they were either moving into or leaving a patrol base.

During their stay on the firebase Bill tried to describe to his new men what it was like in the bush. He went over methods of operation and job responsibility. His objective was to get them as acquainted as possible with life in the jungle, making the transition easier for all of them. The squad leaders reiterated everything he said so, in the LT's mind, they were as ready as they were ever going to be.

On the afternoon of the second day the Third Platoon was patrolling out in front of the Second Platoon and the CP. LT Cook was moving on Bill's left, several hundred meters away. Bill came upon a slow moving, but deep, blue. They had to stop momentarily because there was no apparent place to cross it.

"Two-four tango, two-four, over."

"Two-four tango."

"Roger, tell your pennies to drop their rucks and take five. We've got a blue here that's going to be a bitch to cross if we can't find a shallow point."

"Roger."

"Break, two-four kilo, two-four."

Bill didn't get any response from his trailing squad. He surmised the new RTO was not monitoring the radio like he was supposed to.

"Two-four kilo, two-four kilo, two-four, pick up the horn!'

"Two-four kilo."

"Roger, I want you to monitor that horn all the time. Understand?"

"Roger."

"OK, listen, we've got a deep blue here and it's gonna take a while to find a place to cross it. Tell your sierra lima to have his pennies drop their heavies and take a break."

"Wilco."

Bill took along a few men and they walked about fifty meters up and down the river. There was no safe place to cross. Coming back to the file, he decided to move heavy due east until they found a decent crossing.

"OK, Wayne, let's get it on. Make sure the men know we'll have friendlies on the left for a while.

"Roger."

They began moving again, following the near bank of the river for about one hundred meters. The blue must have made a turn at that point because it disappeared from sight. The LT instructed his point man, a newbie, to turn more toward the right until he picked it up again. The brush was getting really thick and movement was tough. Bill's ruck was continually getting caught on the vines and he was getting more and more frustrated by the minute. The RTO informed him, as they moved, that the Fourth Platoon had come upon some bunkers and were checking them out. Bill kept moving, passing a small clearing. He didn't want to go too far east, for he'd run into LT Cook if he did. All of a sudden the men heard the popping of AK-47s. The sound was coming from the east. Following this was the loud burst of an M-60 and many M-16s. The Fourth Platoon has hit something bad, Bill thought, kneeling down, not sure what to do next. He had his men strung out in one long, snakelike file. It appeared the situation he had hoped wouldn't happen was about to occur. The AK fire became louder and louder, indicating the enemy was moving in Bill's direction, probably retreating from the superior firepower of the Fourth Platoon.

"Wayne, get your squad on line. I have a feeling we're gonna get hit any minute."

Taking the horn from his RTO, Bill told his trailing squads to drop their heavies and stay down. In his mind he knew it would be impossible for Wayne to get his men on line quickly enough. The vegetation was just too thick. All of a sudden the point man opened up with a burst of fire. Dropping the handset, the LT quickly crawled toward him. He was hiding behind a tree, right next to the blue. He said he fired on two gooks and was sure he hit at least one of them.

With a slight sigh of relief, the LT told him to stay down behind the tree and keep his eyes open for any more of them. No sooner had Bill turned back around when his M-60 opened up from midway back in the long file. Running toward the rear, he met his platoon sergeant. He told the LT that Jack and Howie had opened up on two gooks and believed they too had hit one of them.

Trying to think of what to do next, Bill suddenly realized all was quiet again. Remembering that small clearing they had passed, he thought it would be best if they moved back there and set up a hasty perimeter. At least then he would know where his men were. Right now he couldn't tell where the hell they were, let alone where the gooks might be.

He managed to locate everyone and in about ten minutes had them in a perimeter. They were still only a short distance from the river. Bill expected to encounter more gooks so he had his men lying flat on the ground behind their rucks. There wasn't much else to hide behind.

With his hands still shaking and his voice trembling somewhat, he called the CO and told him the situation. Captain Sharp directed all platoons to pop smoke for Max, who was due on station within minutes. The LT's mind relaxed somewhat as the purple smoke filtered up into the clear blue sky from the middle of their perimeter. They hadn't had anyone hurt during the whole melee, thank God.

Shortly thereafter he received instructions to pull back at least five hundred meters. The Fourth Platoon had found additional bunkers and it was decided that jet fighters with their five-hundred-pound bombs would be more effective than Max. Bill pulled back and set up his NDP. Sadly, while in the perimeter, he learned one of LT Cook's men had been killed in the contact that afternoon.

The tentative plan in the morning was to get a resupply of smoke and ammunition. The company would then move back into the contact area. This was something Bill dreaded but knew had to be done. Their missions were recon and destroy, not recon and avoid.

The next morning they received a kick out of supplies and then moved back to the small clearing they had occupied the day before. The LT instructed the men to sit down temporarily to await the arrival of a low bird. In all the excitement of yesterday he had failed to find a place to cross the river. The gooks had done all their firing from the other side. To do a thorough search he had to find a place to cross. The ground in the middle of the perimeter was now stained purple and yellow from the use of many smoke grenades. The men seemed less afraid than they were the day before. They sat quietly awaiting the bird.

About midmorning, leaving two squads in the patrol base, Bill took his remaining squad out to locate a crossing. The low bird came on station shortly thereafter and he spotted the patrol. Bill explained to the pilot his need for a suitable crossing. Buzzing around the area at treetop level, looking and sounding like a giant mosquito, the bird was able to find an old tree that had conveniently fallen across the blue, providing a natural bridge. The pilot told the LT it was just fifty meters from where he was standing. The vegetation was so thick, though, it could have been five meters away and the men probably wouldn't have seen it. Moving in the direction he provided, they located the tree very quickly. The pilot could see no evidence of anyone on the other side but said he would recon by fire just to make sure. Bill radioed back to his patrol base and let them know what was going to happen. While the grunts stood on the near bank the copilot opened up with his M-60 and really fired up the other side. Leaves and branches flew all over the place. The firing ceased moments later and Bill thanked them for their help. He now had only to check out the area immediately on the other side before heading back to the patrol base.

No sooner did one of his men start to walk across the log when an M-16 fired several times from the direction of the patrol base. The Fourth Platoon had been in the process of linking with the Third as Bill searched for a crossing point. With these shots came the fear of a friendly firefight.

"Two-four kilo, two-four, over."

"Two-four kilo."

"Roger, what's going on?"

"The seven-two just shot one of our pennies, over."

"I'm coming right back. Tell the pennies we're coming back. How copy?"

"Solid."

The LT terminated his crossing effort and they literally ran back to the patrol base. The medic was with Bill all this time so they had to get back quickly. One of the LT's assistant gunners was grazed in the stomach by the Fourth Platoon point man. He was the victim of mistaken identity. It wasn't long before they had him on a medevac bird heading back to Bien Hoa. Bill felt sick and angry at the same time. He wanted, so much, to go up to the point man and beat the hell out of him. The guy was obviously shaken up about the whole incident so the LT quickly cleared his mind of that urge. In fact, everyone was on edge from the contact the previous day. LT Cook was very upset too and apologized for the unfortunate accident one of his men had caused. Bill assured Cook he could have done nothing to prevent it. In combat those things occur no matter how careful you try to be.

What a way to spend your last four days in the bush, the LT thought, walking back to his ruck in the middle of the perimeter. Despite what had happened they still had to cross that river and search the other side. Moving heavy this time, the men returned to the fallen tree and carefully, one by one, filed across the blue. Setting up a hasty patrol base, they ate lunch and then planned their search. A little while later an angry CO called Bill and told him they were taking too much time. Captain Sharp decided to personally lead the Fourth Platoon in the search instead. This was fine with the LT. He really didn't want to go back there anyway.

The Fourth Platoon returned about an hour later and reported blood trails about two hundred meters away. This was the area where Bill's men had opened up on the gooks. His newbie point man and veteran gunners had drawn blood with yesterday's fire, just as they claimed. Darkness came quickly so Alpha set up for the night, constructing three separate but close NDPs. Their plan, the next day, was to return to the bunker complex, which the Fourth Platoon had initially found, and destroy the whole thing.

With the help of several engineers who rappelled in by helicopter, three loud cratering charge explosions destroyed the entire complex. The men moved about three hundred meters as a company and set up an NDP around a one-ship LZ. The following day they were scheduled to get logged. It was also the day Bill would relinquish command of his platoon to LT Herzer. LT Sidio would take command of the Second Platoon.

During the night Delta Company, operating four klicks to the south, got in contact with the enemy. Initial reports said they had received mortar fire or possibly B-40 rockets. Enemy movement was reported to be in Alpha's direction. Needless to say, all were on edge that night, particularly the grunts who had experienced the November sixth mortar attack. Luck was with the company, though, for the night remained quiet and serene.

Bill woke up the next morning much less nervous. He truly felt a sense of relief in knowing he was finally going to the rear. The past three days had seemed like an eternity but it was now over. The burden of responsibility, and the associated mental strain, had built up to the point where he was no longer confident in his ability to handle the platoon. It was definitely time for him to step aside and let LT Herzer take over.

The log was like any other he had known, with one exception. He wouldn't be walking back into the jungle with a heavy ruck and a fearful mind anymore. With only a few sorties of the log bird remaining, Bill began walking from one position to another, finding it difficult to say good-bye to his men. He knew he probably wouldn't be seeing most of them again for the rest of his life. He was able, though, to thank each and every one for the tremendous job they had done. Memories of six months in the bush passed before him as they spoke, for each seemed to rekindle an event that was now just a page in history.

Getting word that the final sortie was coming in, the LT had only enough time to grab his gear and quickly shake hands with the CP RTOs. They had worked for months as Bill's RTOs before getting the honor of working in the CP. He felt proud and content at the same time, seeing them together now. His mind held memories of their different arrivals, the times when they sat down in patrol bases going over calls for fire, the times when they just did their jobs. They got to know their platoon leader very well too and were actually able to anticipate his thoughts and actions in the bush. These are the kind of guys, Bill thought, that will keep our country strong and free in the future.

With an empty ruck slung over his shoulder and his M-16 in hand, he headed for the log bird waiting a short distance away. Reaching the open door, he turned and waved to his men one last time.

"Garry Owen," he yelled over the loud noise of the rotor blades, "Garry Owen."

Bill climbed aboard and was lifted out of the jungles of Vietnam. Sitting next to the door gunner, a cold, hard breeze blew in his face. Gazing down to the trees below, he couldn't help but breathe a sigh of relief. It had been a long road, one that definitely had its share of bumps along the way. But somehow he made it. He had accomplished what, maybe deep inside, he really wanted to do. He had commanded an infantry platoon in Vietnam. Never did Bill dream, though, how rewarding this experience would be. Unlike back in August, he now realized he was forever part of a special unit. He was a member of Alpha Company, First of the Seventh Cavalry, First Cavalry Division. For him it was an honor to have worked with the finest, most dedicated men the world has ever known, and share with them an experience they would never forget.

GLOSSARY

Air Cav: air cavalry; helicopter-borne infantry; supported by helicopter gunships.
Airmobile: helicopter-borne infantry.
AK-47: Soviet-manufactured Kalashnikov semiautomatic and fully automatic combat assault rifle, fires a 7.62-mm at six hundred rounds per minute; the basic weapon of the NVA It has a distinctive popping sound.
AO: area of operation in which combat missions are conducted.
artillery: weapons fired from bases within the range of ground operations for their support; examples include howitzers with a caliber of 105mm (105's) and 155mm (155's).
ARVN: Army of the Republic of Vietnam; the South Vietnamese Regular Army.
bourn: a boundary sometimes constructed of dirt or other material to help distinguish secure and insecure territory.
bush: infantry term for the field.
C-4: plastic, putty-textured explosive carried by infantry soldiers; used to blow up bunkers, clear trees for an LZ and even to heat C-rations.

CA: combat assault. The term is used to describe dropping infantry soldiers into an LZ.
Cav: Cavalry; the First Cavalry Division (Airmobile).
Charlie: Viet Cong or NVA.
Chinook: CH-47 cargo helicopter.
CIB: Combat Infantry Badge, an Army award given to infantry soldiers for being under enemy fire in a combat zone.
clacker: a small hand-held firing device for a claymore mine.
claymore: an antipersonnel mine that, when detonated, propelled small steel projectiles in a sixty-degree fan-shaped pattern to a maximum distance of one hundred meters.
CO: commanding officer.
Cobra: an AH-1G attack helicopter, armed with rockets and machine guns.
concertina wire: coiled barbed wire with razor-type ends.
connex container: corrugated metal packing crate, approximately six feet in length.
contact: firing on or being fired upon by the enemy.
CP: command post.
C-rations: combat rations; canned meals for use in the field, usually consisting of a can of some basic course, a can of fruit, a packet of some type of dessert, a packet of powdered coca, sugar, powdered cream, coffee, a small pack of cigarettes, two pieces of chewing gum, and toilet paper.
DEROS: date of expected return from overseas, the day all soldiers in Vietnam were waiting for.
Doc: medic or corpsman.
D-ring: a D-shaped metal snap link used to hold gear together but also used in rappelling from helicopters.

fatigues: standard combat uniform, green in color.

firebase: temporary artillery encampment used for fire support of forward ground operations.

firefight: a battle, or exchange of small arms fire with the enemy.

FO: forward observer, a person attached to a field unit to coordinate the placement of direct or indirect fire from ground, air, and naval forces.

freedom bird: the plane that took soldiers from Vietnam back to the world.

friendly fire: accidental attacks on U.S. or allied soldiers by other U.S. or allied soldiers.

gook: derogatory term for an Asian; derived from Korean slang for "person."

greenline: a bourn or boundary designating secure and insecure territory.

grunt: infantryman or soldier.

gunship: armed helicopter.

hamlet: a small rural village.

HE: high explosive round.

heat tabs: flammable tablet used to heat C-rations. These tablets took a long time to heat the food and gave off harsh fumes, thus C-4 was often used instead.

HHC: headquarters and headquarters company.

hootch: a hut or simple dwelling, either military or civilian.

Huey: nickname for the UH-1 series helicopters.

hump: grunt term to march or walk carrying a heavy rucksack in the field.

I Corps (MR1): the northernmost military region in South Vietnam.

II Corps (MR2): the Central Highlands military region in South Vietnam.
III Corps (MR3): the densely populated, fertile military region between Saigon and the Highlands.
IV Corps (MR4): the marshy Mekong Delta southernmost military region.
insert: to be deployed into a tactical area by helicopter.
JP: jungle penetrator, an L-shaped device used to evacuate wounded by helicopter when the individual still had use of his arms.
KIA: killed in action.
Kit Carson scout: former Viet Cong who acted as guides for U.S. military units.
klick: one kilometer.
lance: number of personnel in the field.
LBJ: Long Binh Jail, a military stockade in the city of Long Binh.
loach: an OH-6A light observation helicopter with one pilot and one or two gunner/observers.
log: resupply of food, water, ammunition, and other requested items of equipment.
log bird: resupply helicopter.
LP: listening post, usually set up outside the perimeter, away from the main body of personnel, that provided an early warning system against attack.
LT: lieutenant, leader of a platoon of personnel; grunts used the letters LT for short to refer to their leader.
LRRPs: long-range reconnaissance patrol rations (dehydrated food packages that replaced C-rations).
LZ: landing zone; usually a small clearing secured temporarily during a CA and for the landing of resupply helicopters;

some become more permanent and eventually become base camps or firebases.

M-16: the standard U.S. military rifle used in Vietnam from 1966 on. It was the successor to the M-14.

M-60: the standard lightweight machine gun used by U.S. forces in Vietnam.

M-79: a U.S. military hand-held grenade launcher.

M-203: a combination M-16 and grenade launcher.

medevac: medical evacuation from the field by helicopter.

Minigun: rapid-fire machine gun with multibarrels that was electronically controlled, capable of firing up to six thousand rounds per minute, primarily used on choppers and other aircraft.

mortar: a weapon consisting of three parts: a steel tube, base plate, and tripod. A round was dropped in the tube, striking a firing pin, causing the projectile to leave the tube at a high angle.

MP: military police.

MPC: military payment certificates.

napalm: a jellied petroleum substance which burned fiercely, used against enemy personnel.

NDP: night defensive position or perimeter.

number one: the best.

number ten: the worst.

NVA: North Vietnamese Army.

OCS: officer candidate school.

OP: observation post.

pathfinder: someone specifically trained in ground-to-air communication.

perimeter: outer limits of a military position.

point man: the forward man or element on a combat patrol.

POL: aircraft petroleum (fuel), oils and lubricant.
pop smoke: to ignite a smoke grenade to signal an aircraft.
POW: prisoner of war.
Purple Heart: U.S. military decoration awarded to any member of the Armed Forces wounded by enemy action.
PZ: pick up zone.
push: radio frequency.
R&R: rest and recreation. Two types: a three-day in-country (e.g., Vung Tau) and a seven-day out-of-country vacation (e.g., Thailand, Australia, Hawaii, Hong Kong).
Rangers: Army elite commandos and infantry specially trained for reconnaissance and combat missions.
Ready Reaction Force: A unit set up in advance to come to the aid of another unit under enemy fire.
recon: reconnaissance.
rigid litter: a cot-like board used for helicopter evacuations of wounded individuals who did not have use of their arms.
RTO: radio telephone operator.
ruck/rucksack: backpack issued to infantry in Vietnam to carry food, water, and equipment.
S-1: Personnel Administration.
S-2: Intelligence Administration.
S-3: Operations Administration.
S-4: Supply Administration.
S-5: Civil Affairs.
sapper: a Viet Cong or NVA solder who got inside the perimeter, armed with explosives such as satchel charges.
satchel charges: pack used by the enemy containing explosives, dropped or thrown and generally more powerful than a grenade.

shack: process of coding information before transmission by radio.
short: tour of duty being close to completion.
short-timer: soldier nearing the end of his tour in Vietnam.
shrapnel: pieces of metal sent flying by an explosive round.
sit rep: situation report filed with S-2 when a contact occurred or when important information was obtained.
slack man: the second man back on a patrol, directly behind the point man.
slick: a UH-1 helicopter used for transporting troops in tactical air assault operations.
smoke grenade: a grenade that released brightly colored smoke. Used for signaling choppers.
TAC Officer: officer charged with the training, advising, and counseling of individuals.
TOC: tactical operations center.
Top: a top sergeant (e.g., field first sergeant).
tracer: a round of ammunition chemically treated to glow so that its flight can be followed.
trip flare: a ground flare triggered by a trip wire. Used to notify the approach of the enemy. It was often used in conjunction with the placement of a claymore mine.
UH-1H: a Huey helicopter.
URS: unidentified radio signal.
VC: Viet Cong.
Victor Charlie: the Viet Cong; the enemy.
Viet Cong: South Vietnamese Communist.
VR: visual reconnaissance.
wake-up: the last day of a soldier's Vietnam tour. An example for six days: five days and a wake-up.

white phosphorus: an explosive round from artillery, mortars, rockets, or grenades. Also a type of aerial bomb. When the rounds exploded a huge puff of white smoke would appear from the burning phosphorus. The round was used as a marking or an incendiary device.
WP/Wilson Pickett/Willy Peter: white phosphorus.
wood line: trees at the edge of a field, LZ, or firebase.
the world: the United States.
XO: executive officer; the second in command of a military unit.

Made in the USA
Charleston, SC
17 March 2010